31 DAYS OF

MINDFUL PROVERBS

HEALING WORDS FOR THE SOUL

31 DAYS OF
MINDFUL PROVERBS

HEALING WORDS FOR THE SOUL

Latoya A. Delmadge

EQUIP PRESS

Colorado Springs

31 DAYS OF
MINDFUL PROVERBS

First Edition: 2019
31 Days of Mindful Proverbs / Latoya A. Delmadge
Paperback ISBN: 978-1-946453-59-4
eBook ISBN: 978-1-946453-59-4

EQUIP PRESS

Colorado Springs

ENDORSEMENTS

Latoya has united her background in psychology with her deep faith and biblical background to guide the reader through a journey to realign our thoughts to God's perfect blueprint of principles and purpose for our lives. Each day's reading challenges the reader through probing questions which, if conscientiously answered, will promote our spiritual growth. This unique and succinct book is one to return to repeatedly to reevaluate and draw you to greater depths of relationship with God and higher purpose for Him.

REV. SHARON FRANK
Director of Encourage Ministry Women for the New York Ministry
Network of the Assemblies of God

One constant in life is change. *31 Days of Mindful Proverbs* is a practical and spiritual guidebook as to how to deal with change. I highly recommend this book for anyone dealing with the ups and downs of living in a world that you are in but not necessarily of.

Many important lessons in life are explained in the book of Proverbs. But extracting those lessons can be hard. This book provides an everyday explanation of these life lessons in common terms that we all can identify with.

Although it is obvious that Latoya Delmadge, the author of this amazing book, is a well-educated person, I enjoyed the nonacademic approach to very deep concepts of psychology and sociology.

If one has a demanding and challenging life, I definitely recommend for them to read this book.

This book reminds me that on the other side of hurting is healing, and reading this positive influence is a core requirement of any healing process.

CARRIÉ SOLAGES
NASSAU COUNTY Legislator and Attorney

PREFACE

Sitting with my patient in an outpatient mental health clinic where I work, she tells me that she is severely depressed and wants to feel better but cannot shake her feelings. She is eager to be happy and live a life filled with joy and happiness, but she daily finds herself in this "dark place." Throughout the assessment stage, I learn that she is a born-again Christian and has had a relationship with God for a significant part of her life. Yet her mental health is an area that she just cannot overcome. I probe further to understand her thought process. She lays out all the negative thoughts that go through her mind throughout the day, which in turn affects her mood and behavior, leading to lack of productivity on her job and healthy relationships with others. She could not recall a pattern of positive thinking. Then I noticed the influx of believers who were seeking therapy for the same presenting problems: depression and anxiety; the complaints of just not being happy and finding complete fulfillment, despite their relationship with God. I began to think more about living a successful, fruitful life and the ingredients for such a concoction, and the Lord made it completely clear to me; He showed me the mind. The Lord showed me that we have the power to change our life through our thought patterns.

Having a spiritual lens through Scripture and teaching, my understanding of depression and anxiety has deepened beyond my educational knowledge and trainings. This information and insight is used to bring mental healing to my patients and start the journey to more productive thought patterns. The *31 Days of Mindful Proverbs* journey is not complete after thirty-one days, it is just beginning.

The content of this book is meant to motivate readers to be more aware of their thought process and identify how their thoughts have shaped their lives. I hope to bring awareness to how we can use our minds as the catalyst for greatness and comprehensive life-growth.

For a long time, I was taught that if you want to see change in your life, just pray. And if nothing happens, pray some more. If you still don't see results, pray harder and longer. What I've learned is that you have a responsibility to exercise what God has already given you and if your situation does not change, then you need to change. Many people are not aware of thought patterns that have led to behavioral patterns in their lives that they have probably inherited through vicarious learning. God wants to break maladaptive patterns, and awareness of those patterns will begin with your engagement with this book.

The psychodynamic perspective theory is very relevant in that it sheds light on the experiences we have in our early years of life and how our experiences and interactions with others shape our character, the way we think, and how we view the world around us. According to *Psychology Today*, psychodynamic theory states that events in our childhood have a great influence on our adult lives, shaping our personality. Events that occur in childhood can remain in the unconscious and cause problems as adults.

This book, *31 Days of Mindful Proverbs,* will propel you to begin the process of change in cycles of thinking that have caused undesirable feelings, unacceptable behaviors, and stagnation in your life and even social conflict due to fear, depression, anxiety, and personality disorders. As a reader, you will be propelled to think about what you are thinking about.

As Sigmund Freud said, "The unconscious mind is the primary source of human behavior. Like an iceberg, the most important part of the mind is the part you cannot see."[1]

I challenge you to be vulnerable as you read this book and use the personal reflections to assess yourself after each reading. Know that God is going to change you, starting with your awareness. God wants to push you to another level and He is preparing His people for greatness; this book is one of many resources that God will use to perfect His work in you. God wants His people to experience comprehensive health, and your mental health is a part of that. The third book of John chapter 1 verse 2 says, "Beloved, I wish above all things that thou mayest prosper and be in health, even as thy soul prospereth." Cheers to your journey of comprehensive health and mindfulness.

---

[1] Saul McLeod, "Psychodynamic Approach," 2017, https://www.simplypsychology.org/psychodynamic.html.

HEALING WORDS
FOR THE SOUL

The actions that we produce are driven by our thoughts. Before we make any steps in a particular direction, it is best that we hold ourselves accountable by processing our very own thoughts.

The Word of God teaches us how powerful and influential our thought patterns are; they direct the course of our life. Proverbs 23:7 says, "For as he thinketh in his heart, so is he." Does this mean that if we think of a chicken, we are in actuality a chicken? Absolutely not. But if we focus on chicken constantly and fix our thoughts on our longing and desire for chicken, we will engage in eating it very often and can rightly be defined as "chicken lovers." Let's take for example the illustration of lusting after someone in our heart, continually. As the thought of lust comes in our mind, it is our responsibility to process why we thought of lust, how we plan to respond to this thought, and whether this thought will become a recurring thought. If we have thoughts of low self-esteem, we do not have to be defined as a person with low self-esteem or allow these thoughts to control us. We claim and utilize the power within us by countering our thoughts with faithfulness and confidence. As powerful, thinking human beings, we have to master the art of directing our thought patterns into a fruitful, positive, and productive direction. Yes! We can accomplish this task, but it will require some work.

We all are faced with maladaptive thoughts at times, but we all have the ability to channel our thoughts and direct our actions. The initial stage of mindfulness is awareness. Awareness is extremely significant because, before we are able to challenge a thought process, we have to be aware of that thought and judge its content. Let's go back to thoughts of lust. A great place to start is to first identify that the thoughts we are having are lustful. After our thought is identified, we then weigh whether it is productive or destructive, which is guided firstly by our belief system and moral standard. Any thought we have should be judged by asking ourselves the question: Is it maladaptive or worth adapting; is it life bearing or marked with death? Ask yourself: What will happen if I water this thought and what kind of fruit will it produce? Whatever results we are looking for, we should move in that direction with that thought.

If we experience thoughts of depression, as we all do from time to time, we know that these thoughts are destructive and maladaptive. They are marked with death, as they do not yield any life. If we take a look at individuals who have watered thoughts of depression and weigh the results or the fruit that comes from their thoughts, we see the fruit of suicide, we see the fruit of low quality of life, we see the fruit of strained family dynamics. The list can go on and on as the results vary from person to person, but the results are never positive. At this point, we are aware; before moving any further in countering maladaptive thoughts, we must be aware. Without awareness, there will be no change.

Maladaptive, unproductive thoughts will no longer keep us bound if we decide to take a step toward countering them and reprogramming our thought patterns. The Word of God is the most powerful tool to use in our mindfulness journey. Other tools are also helpful, but we will focus primarily on God's Word, and other resources will be used as support. The Word of God directs on things that are good and acceptable. John 6:63 says, "It is the spirit that quickeneth; the flesh profiteth nothing: the words that I speak unto you, they are spirit, and they are life." Therefore, we have something substantial to measure our thoughts with and judge based on our belief, and because it is life, it will cause us to live. This battle over the thoughts of our mind is not a one-time victory, but rather a constant war that we have to fight, and with God, we are guaranteed the victory.

Spiritual Food for Thought:

Proverbs 4:23—Keep thy heart with all diligence; for out of it are the issues of life.

PERSONAL REFLECTION:

Question: What patterns of thinking have led to feelings of depression and low self-esteem in your life? Think back into your childhood. How have encounters in your childhood influenced your thought pattern around low self-esteem?

2

I am what I think. People cannot see our thoughts, but they judge our thoughts by our actions. On this day, we are challenged to be mindful of what message we send to others by our actions.

I remember when I was sixteen, my mother gave birth to my little sister, Simone. I always prayed for a sister but I wanted her sooner rather than later; I desired to be close in age. So, despite the joy that I felt, I also felt some resentment because I wanted to have a sister who I could grow with. I felt as though I was way past her in age. What could we possibly talk about and what places could we go together? These are thoughts I had then. My thoughts of resentment were quite evident in my behaviors because my family members always said that I was jealous of my sister, which I absolutely was not. At the time, I really could not identify my feelings, much less control my thoughts.

Growing up, there was always a rift between my sister and me that could not really be explained, and I had to be mindful in order to improve the relationship. As I matured, I realized that I was struggling with desire versus reality. My desire was for a sister who I could relate to and connect with on my level, but in reality, I had a sister who I had to instruct, guide, and protect. I later realized that I had to work harder on my thoughts about my sister and what I originally expected and work on what is and appreciate what is.

Apparently, others could see my maladaptive thoughts through my actions, which were not quite visible to me, and my sister sensed that tension, which hindered her ability to securely attach to me.

At that time, I was not mindful of my thoughts and how they were exhibited through my behaviors. Frustration and disappointment were my feelings at the time, and so I was impatient with her, harsh, and at times dismissive.

Now that I have studied the art of mindfulness, I can take responsibility for my thoughts and be more active in adjusting my thoughts to more positive ways of thinking. And ultimately, others will see my thoughts through my actions. We cannot change the past us, but we have the power to improve the future us. Presently, I have learned to acknowledge my sister more and deal with her utilizing the virtue of patience. Our relationship is not one hundred percent and she is still not close to me in age, but the rift that we once had is no longer there. I have worked on finding ways to connect with her and ironically, as the years go by, I realize that we have more in common than I thought. However, I first had to be aware of how I was thinking and what types of behaviors I was exhibiting. I also had to recognize how my actions influenced our relationship. It was not a good result and I took the responsibility to change it, but the change first started in my mind.

Once we identify our thoughts and point out their origin, we can then move forward in countering our thoughts and reprogramming our brain to think differently. I used to think of my sister as a burden, but now I see her as an asset to my life. As a result of my thoughts, I am sure that others see a positive response as well. Our abilities to reframe situations in our lives will be extremely beneficial to our perception, feelings, and behaviors.

If we identify as followers of Jesus Christ, we have the responsibility to act when we are aware of strained relationships in our lives. Matthew 5:23–24 says, "Therefore if thou bring thy gift to the altar, and there rememberest that thy brother hath ought against thee; Leave there thy gift before the altar, and go thy way; first be reconciled to thy brother, and then come and offer thy gift." We will always experience misunderstandings with people in our lives, but if we program our brains to conform to thoughts of peace and reconciliation, we will be more confident in how we will handle conflicts with others when the time comes. All we need is an aware and yielded mind.

Spiritual Food for Thought:

Proverbs 23:7—For as he thinks in his heart, so is he. "Eat and drink!" he says to you, but his heart is not with you. (NKJV)

PERSONAL REFLECTION:

Question: What are some strained relationships in your life? What role have you played in that dynamic? Identify your thoughts in relation to your actions.

Elevation occurs long before an opportunity; it begins with the state of our hearts. It is only with a good heart that elevation can be sustained. If our heart is not good ground, we will end up right back where we started.

How many times in the Word of God have we seen great leaders fall? So many. Yet still, we make the same mistakes they made and fall into the same trap of pride. I am reminded of a pastor who God used mightily when I was growing up. He was so anointed and when he preached, you felt heaven in the room; I mean powerful! But there was a side to him that was prideful: his speech, his walk, even his look. Now, I believe as people of God, we should have a sense of confidence in who we are and who we represent, but we should not conduct ourselves in a way that makes us unreachable. We should not make others feel uncomfortable in their mediocre ways but comfortable enough to know that if we can, they can. This man of God that I speak of eventually fell and experienced great humiliation. I do not rejoice at his result, but I am aware of the results of pride and am very mindful of thoughts of pride in my mind that I quickly reprogram and redirect, continually.

One of my most favorite quotes by Maya Angelou states: "I've learned that people will forget what you said, people will forget what you did, but people will never forget how you made them feel." Chances are that if we have pride in our hearts and if we have a sense of arrogance, others around us will feel belittled. We may not purposefully make them feel this way, but because of our elevated thoughts of ourselves, our actions will naturally follow suit.

A beautiful attribute of King David was his ability to point all things back to God and be humble despite his many victories. The Lord said that David was a man after His own heart. What does that even mean? David had a heart that was malleable. When corrected, he took heed. David's pattern of pointing glory to God kept him in a humble state of mind, even in his elevated status as king of Israel. David's humble attribute was cultivated way before he became king.

As I read how David conducted himself with King Saul, he was already being groomed for a leadership position; he was purposed to be king. This is evident in his ability to respect authority. In the book of 1 Samuel, we see Saul's never-ending pursuit to kill David because jealousy resided in Saul's heart; Saul's thoughts were in a destructive place. Despite Saul's pursuit after David, who was Saul's greatest warrior and supporter, David remained submitted to Saul and honored him even in Saul's death.

David did not honor Saul because he wanted to be recognized by him. David honored Saul because he had a conviction in his heart pertaining to dishonoring God's chosen and anointed. David's heart was always in a good place, even before he was elevated to his position as king. If we read the book of 2 Samuel chapter 1, we see how David judged the Amalekite who proclaimed to have taken the life of Saul. Even though the account of Saul's death to David by the Amalekite was false, David believed what he heard and judged the Amalekite for destroying God's anointed.

Saul was completely different than David, however. In 1 Samuel 10, God anointed Saul as king, but we see later in the book of 1 Samuel the state of Saul's heart was not able to sustain his position as king. If Saul had a heart of submission before he was appointed king, he would have been able to respond to the challenges that came his way more wisely. In 1 Samuel 15, God commanded Saul to smite Amalek and destroy *all* that he had. However, Saul disobeyed God and spared Agag, the best of the sheep, oxen, fatlings, lambs, and all that was good. Not only did Saul disobey God, but when he was confronted by Samuel about carrying out the task that God gave him, he lied and said that he did all that God commanded. Saul's character was flawed.

In our condition of submission, we are able to acquire valuable attributes that are needed in our place of elevation. If you fail to carry the necessary attributes of good character with you, you will fall. When David became king, he too sinned, by having sexual relations with Bathsheba, who was the wife of one of David's faithful soldiers, Uriah. The difference between David and Saul is that when God pointed out David's sin, he was honest and repented. David had a heart of humility and as a result, God was able to restore and sustain him.

The thoughts that we have around things in our lives that are not good for us are not meant to break us, but they are rather meant to build us. Our character is formed when we respond readily and humbly to areas in our lives that need to be changed. Do not ignore that thought around an area that God is trying to change in your life. God is touching that area and many more because He is preparing you for elevation. Some thoughts of conviction may sound like "hmm, that was not very nice" or "what you did was pretty bad" or even "I feel bad about what I just said." Don't ignore that thought. Be aware of that sound thought, process it, judge it, and respond well.

Spiritual Food for Thought:

Psalm 139:23–24—Search me, O God, and know my heart: try me, and know my thoughts: And see if there be any wicked way in me, and lead me in the way everlasting.

PERSONAL REFLECTION:

Question: What are your thought patterns of yourself in relation to your accomplishments or life status? Can you identify any form of pride in your life?

4

Good ground will always yield growth to great things in our lives. It is important to be mindful of the seeds that we plant in our hearts as well as the hearts of others.

When we desire to experience greatness in our lives, we first have to plant seeds of greatness. The state of our hearts is extremely important. The Word of God says in Galatians 6:7, "Be not deceived; God is not mocked: for whatsoever a man soweth, that shall he also reap." Whatever we sow, whether it be in word or deed, at some point in our lives, it will come back to us. What is oftentimes overlooked is the length of time in reaping. At times we think that we will reap a harvest right away, but the Bible does not give us a specific time to expect our harvest. The Lord just promises that we will in fact reap whatsoever we sow. If we sow kindness, we will reap kindness. If we sow hate, we will reap hate. If we sow positive thoughts and words in the lives of those around us, we are just setting ourselves up for positive things and success to occur in our own lives.

Parents who are not able to give their children an inheritance of wealth, property, or shares but are able to pass down principles of kindness, love, gratitude, and respect can position their offspring to reach great levels in life that those who do not have these qualities would not be able to sustain. My mother is a woman who planted seeds of faithfulness and good character in me. Not just by what she told me, but rather by how she lived. Vicarious learning is extremely powerful. I glean a lot of valuable lessons on life through the life that she lives as well as the sharing of her stories and experiences with me.

My mother shared the story with me about when she needed her front porch fixed. At the time, money was not readily available and financial hard times were upon our family. The desire to have her front porch fixed was steady on her heart, but that desire was oftentimes dismissed by the realities of our finances. One day, she noticed that our neighbor was fixing her front porch. My mother recalls the day when she came in the house and was so joyful that our neighbor was able to fix her front porch, and she thought to herself, *Well, if her porch is fixed and she is directly next to me, it will make mine look at least a little decent.* She praised God and thanked Him for the blessing He was releasing on our neighbor, and the praise was genuine. Within a couple of weeks, the same contractors who worked on my neighbor's property, without either of my parents approaching them, willingly offered to fix our front porch at a very reasonable price. My mother's heart was good ground and as a result, she reaped a great blessing in that time of her life. The pattern of greatness has the potential to continue, given that you continue to prepare a place for it to grow.

As my mother rejoiced with her neighbor, she was creating the space for God to do something great for her, which He did. The seed of contentment and altruism was not only fruitful in my mother's situation, but it kept growing as it was passed to me, and I continue to plant it in my life as I see the beneficial results of it. And it will not stop with me, but I pass it on to you and will surely teach my children its value.

Spiritual Food for Thought:

Isaiah 55:11—So shall my word be that goeth forth out of my mouth: it shall not return unto me void, but it shall accomplish that which I please, and it shall prosper in the thing whereto I sent it.

PERSONAL REFLECTION:

Question: What seeds have you been sowing in your heart by the thoughts you meditate on? What kind of harvest are you expecting from those thoughts? What do you feel convicted to change?

5

We have the power to accomplish and achieve whatever we believe. Our thought is the road that leads to our dreams.

Whatever we spend our time thinking about becomes the driving force for our actions. For example, when we are driving a vehicle and we focus our attention on a specific direction, whether it be to the left of us or the right of us, the car we are driving automatically goes in the direction of our focus. The same concept is true in the way we think lining up with our actions, which directs the course of our lives. We are able to achieve every dream and ambition that we set our minds to; the only barrier that can hinder our progress is our thoughts.

God has already declared that He has good thoughts for us and our future. However, there are forces in this world that want to keep us back from seeing God's perfect plan. So, we encounter things in life that are meant to discourage us and make us believe that we are not capable or that we are not meant for good. For some of us, it is parents who never encouraged us or someone in our lives who took advantage of us. I've heard of many traumatic childhood experiences that have shaped individuals' lives, and without purposeful mindfulness and a different outlook on their situations, they could easily be held back from moving into their destiny. Their mind was stuck. Stuck in their past circumstances. Stuck in believing that they were not created for greatness. Stuck in their trauma.

Thought processes that were revealed by the declaration of the lips were: "with all that has happened to me, it is evident that I was not meant for good"; "my mother always told me that I would end up a single mother struggling just like her, and that's exactly what happened"; "I've tried and tried and I still end up in the same place; that's a sign that I am not meant for more." The problem is not that life was destined to work against you; the enlightenment is that, because you've been shaped to think of yourself based on your experiences, your actions just fulfilled those very thought patterns. Your situation has become a self-fulfilling prophecy. According to an article published by Positive Psychology Program, "When our beliefs and expectations influence our behavior at the subconscious level, we are enacting what is known as a self-fulfilling prophecy."[2] Our situations have been shaped by our thoughts.

How do we change the course of these thought patterns? We already identified the first stage of awareness. Now we are challenged to replace the negative thought with more positive thoughts and reprogram our thought process. But first we must firmly believe in the ability of our thoughts coming to pass, and purpose must be found in our past disappointments. If we believe that God has a great plan and purpose for our lives, we start with that belief. Romans 8:28 says, "And we know that all things work together for good to them that love God, to them who are the called according to his purpose."

Reprogramming our minds requires repetition. I am not surprised that God commanded His people to meditate on His words day and night. To believe in our new purposeful life process in God requires us to continually remind ourselves of what His Word says with convicting belief. At one point in our life, we believed that success is not for us; no one else in our family succeeded. But now that we believe on the

---

[2]   Courtney Ackerman, "Self-Fulfilling Prophecy in Psychology: 10 Examples and Definition," *Positive Psychology Program*, May 1, 2018, https://positivepsychologyprogram.com/self-fulfilling-prophecy/.

power of God and His great plan for us, we now believe that whatever we set our minds to do, according to the will of God, we will do. Every time we encountered a challenge, in our past thought process, we would think that it is too hard for us and give up easily, but now that we are on the road of mindfulness and reprogramming our thoughts through the Word of God, when we encounter a challenge we think, "I can do all things through Christ who strengthens me" (Philippians 4:13, NKJV). For decades, researchers have concluded that the human brain could not be regenerated in adulthood. However, recent discoveries proved otherwise. I am not surprised about this discovery because God already commanded His people to be transformed by the renewing of our minds (Romans 12:2).

When we define ourselves by who God says we are, our state of mind gives us confidence, and with this confidence, we step out with boldness and begin to follow the necessary steps that lead to our expected end. We have the ability to walk in our dreams, the great destiny that was already declared before the world was even formed. So go ahead, move forward in that dream and believe what God said.

Spiritual Food for Thought:

Ephesians 1:4—According as he hath chosen us in him before the foundation of the world, that we should be holy and without blame before him in love.

PERSONAL REFLECTION:

Question: What dreams have you felt insecure in pursuing? How have your thoughts held you back from moving forward with your life goals and ambitions?

6

I can go as far as my mind allows and accomplish as much as I can dream and believe in my heart.

Yes! We continue to be mindful about dreams and visions. There are spiritual forces that are designed to keep us back from achieving our purpose; that is their purpose. If that is their purpose, these spiritual forces spend all their time functioning in their calling. If we are not firmly rooted and grounded in our belief of who God created us to be and our function in Him, we will be defeated. One way of staying focused and motivated in our goals is through the use of vision boards. A vision board is simply any type of board that reflects the ambitions and goals of the visionary. For example, if I am aspiring to be a politician, I may create a board filled with pictures of politicians I respect and aspire to be like. I may have pictures of political activities that I look forward to being involved in and words that reflect my cause and political views. Vision boards are a powerful tool to fuel motivation and build faith. The purpose of creating a vision board is to frame our dreams and life ambitions. Research has proven that if our dreams and future goals are clear and the planning process is outlined, the possibility of achieving them is greater. But the first step is to have a clear dream or vision.

The last vision board I created was in 2015, and the truth is that it is about time for me to start setting some more clear goals for myself. On my vision board, I reflected my desire to, first and foremost, grow spiritually; then complete my master's degree; have another baby, preferably a girl; and practice a healthy lifestyle (diet, exercise, and social life). My entire vision was fulfilled. I was able to complete my master's degree, I gave birth to a baby girl the following year, and I've made progressive steps to eating healthy and maintaining a vibrant social life. My walk with the Lord tops it all; there is such depth, revelation, and awareness of who I am because of Him. The Lord completes my entire life and gives me new visions and desires.

As we seek after God, He leads our desires based on what He has planned for us, and His plans are always great. God gives us the plan and steps that will lead to the accomplishment of our goals. A very dear patient of mine introduced me to a quote by Antoine de Saint-Exupéry that says, "A goal without a plan is just a wish. God gives us the goal and He instructs us exactly how we should plan to reach it."

Do not limit yourself; more so, do not limit God. The Word of God says in Isaiah 55:9, "For as the heavens are higher than the earth, so are my ways higher than your ways, and my thoughts than your thoughts." God wants you to dream and create space for Him to outdo your biggest desires. I always tell the Lord, "You are bigger than my thoughts and will do better than I can even imagine."

When I graduated with my master's degree, I don't know why, but God put in my heart the desire to obtain a leadership position in my career. I started praying and asking God for a supervisor's position because I had been working in my current position at the time for more than three years and gained an ample amount of experience. God gave me even greater than what I asked for; He gave me a director's position! In my position as a director, God uses me to pour into the lives of my staff, who are receptive, as well as other colleagues and vice versa. This is just one of countless accounts of God going above and beyond my dreams, and He will do the same for you.

Spiritual Food for Thought:

Proverbs 29:18—Where there is no vision, the people perish: but he that keepeth the law, happy is he.

PERSONAL REFLECTION:

Question: What purpose has God birthed in you? Are you walking in your purpose? If not, what thoughts and feelings are holding you back?

7

The words that you speak are life. Speak that which you would like to see come to pass in your life, according to the promises that God has recorded in His Word, and wait patiently for the fulfillment.

As we master the stage of awareness, we are then challenged to believe in God for greatness. When we do our part in allowing our lives to be transformed by the renewing of our minds, God rewards us according to our obedience. At this point, we have a boldness to stand on God's Word and declare what He promised us. We know that Romans 8:1 says, "There is therefore now no condemnation to them which are in Christ Jesus, who walk not after the flesh, but after the Spirit." If our thoughts are not Spirit-led, then our actions will not be led by the Spirit. When we are not walking in the Spirit of God, we do not have the boldness and the confidence to proclaim His Word. Walking habitually in the flesh is completely different than stepping out of the Spirit and responding in the flesh for some situations. A habit is practiced unconsciously because our minds are trained to think a certain way and, therefore, our behaviors based on our thought patterns come naturally.

Thank God for awareness. When we are aware of our maladaptive patterns of thinking and respond to the Holy Spirit's prompting to conform our thoughts to God's Word, we begin to have a sense of longing for the promises of God and the enemy has no foothold over us because we responded in obedience. Obedience keeps us in alignment with God. We then have the confidence of who we are in God and His purpose for our lives void of condemnation because we are in the Spirit and respond freely to the Spirit of God working in us. God has already written our story and success, and as we mature in Him, He reveals His secrets and plans to us. His expectation is that we proclaim what He has revealed to us and promised us. Stand on His promises.

I have a practice of speaking to myself in the mirror every morning. After getting dressed and applying my makeup, I speak to the inner part of me and tell myself who I am and what it is that I will accomplish each day. More so, I speak into my future. I say: "Latoya, you are the head and not the tail, you are above and not beneath, you are more than a conqueror through Christ Jesus. The favor of the Lord is upon your life. No weapon that is formed against you shall prosper and every tongue that riseth up against you shall be condemned. Surely goodness and mercy shall follow you every day of your life and you shall fulfill the purpose of God for your life today, in Jesus' name, amen." I say this every day, and every day, I see the fulfillment of my words. God has always led me in a way where I start out at the lowest position and am elevated to a high position. But I've learned that the lesson that the Lord continues to teach me is humility.

The more you tell yourself what you want to see, the more you begin to believe it and the likelihood it will become a reality. Your actions will begin to be led by your thoughts and beliefs; your thoughts and actions will be in alignment. The Word of God says in Colossians 3:2, "Set your affections on things above, not on things on the earth." Why would God encourage us to think about heavenly things and hold them in much higher esteem and regard than earthly things? Well, where your heart and mind are, your actions will follow. Whatever you start to prophesy propels your actions, which yields to that which you believed in your heart. Also, when we are led by the Spirit of God, He reveals His plans for our lives and we are not being led by our own human ambitions. God's plans and man's plans makes a differ- ence. God has no obligation to honor the plans of man. But He has a commitment to His Word. Psalm 138:2 says, "I will worship toward thy holy temple, and praise thy name for thy lovingkindness and for thy truth: for thou hast magnified thy word above all thy name."

I oftentimes tell my patients to speak to themselves and say what they would like to feel and believe. For those who struggle with their self-confidence, I encourage them to speak out loud that they are powerful, talented, and able to do great things. That they are beautifully and wonderfully made. Surely, over time, they start to engage in tasks that at one point they would not even think of, much less do. And when they give me their report, I remind them of their step to believing that started with their open declaration to themselves. You are your greatest and most powerful affirmer.

Spiritual Food for Thought:

Proverbs 18:21—Death and life are in the power of the tongue: and they that love it shall eat the fruit thereof.

PERSONAL REFLECTION:

Question: What has been your practice in declaring God's promises? Has condemnation influenced your motivation to confess and stand on God's promises?

Being visible of the good in others gives light to the greatness in you. A clouded heart fogs judgment and positive perspectives.

What are those processes and behaviors that keep us stagnant and do not encourage growth in parts of our lives? Being critical and judgmental of others can surely hinder growth in our lives and cause anxiety. How do judgmental thoughts trigger feelings of anxiety? Well, when we have a pattern of creating expectations in our mind for others as to how they should act, respond, and behave, we not only carry that weight of expectations for them but for ourselves as well. When our judgment for others is high, we in turn place that same judgment on ourselves. In the process of demanding others to measure up, we too feel the overwhelming need to measure up. Matthew 7:2 says, "For in the same way you judge others, you will be judged, and with the measure you use, it will be measured to you" (NIV).

Anxiety is a diagnosis wherein people experience various kinds of fears: fear of failure, fear of speaking in public, fear of people, fear of not living up to the expectations of others, fear of places and things, just to name a few. And most times when I speak with patients about their anxieties and I ask them about their thoughts of others, their expectations for others are usually very high. There is very little room for mistakes or hiccups, which is also the parallel version of their perspective for themselves and the situations that surround their life. There is always good in every situation and if we seek for that good, we will find it. The opposite is also true; if we look for the bad in people and situations, we will find it. This leads us to a deeper thought. If we can only see the negative in situations, our thoughts are also negative, which will affect our judgment and actions. Awareness around this context is meant to challenge us to search for patterns of thinking that need to change in order to find freedom in this part of our life.

Have you ever had an adverse feeling for a person you just did not like? How did you view that person? How did you judge their actions? Think about your thoughts of them. I can note times when someone was not in my favorable eye; everything they did was wrong, even when it was right. I viewed them as corrupt in their actions, and that was because my own thoughts of them were corrupt; my judgment was compromised because of my subjective thoughts. Here is the beautiful side. There is hope of change. Once I started to find the good in people, I noticed that my own level of anxieties and stress subsided. The same report was relayed to me by some of my patients who I treat for anxiety.

We cannot work on patterns of thinking around being critical and judgmental if we are not aware of how we are thinking first. The practice of changing our pattern of thinking is challenging and requires work. We have to be motivated and willing to change.

The Word of God says in Philippians 4:8, "Finally, brethren, whatsoever things are true, whatsoever things are honest, whatsoever things are just, whatsoever things are pure, whatsoever things are lovely, whatsoever things are of good report; if there be any virtue, and if there be any praise, think on these things." Philippians 2:3 says, "Let nothing be done through strife or vainglory; but in lowliness of mind let each esteem other better than themselves." If we are struggling with anxiety and experience a high degree of fear, chances are, there is a lack of love and empathy in our heart for others. A part of mindfulness practice that is very effective is the ability to extend compassion and empathy to others in order to affect levels of compassion and empathy for ourselves. What we want for ourselves has to first start with what we give to others. When we begin to extend patience to others and support as they experience their journey of evolving, we will find that our journey is less taxing on our emotions and we will experience less anxiety. The decrease in our anxiety will come from thoughts that we are all human and make mistakes and are forever learning and growing. Part of our growth is mixed with failures and hiccups. We are not perfect in ourselves, but we are perfected in Him. Proverbs 24:16 says, "For a just man falleth seven times, and riseth up again: but the wicked shall fall into mischief." We will fall, but the difference is that we have the strength to get back up. Encourage those around you to get back up and praise their efforts to rise and not give up.

Spiritual Food for Thought:

1 John 4:18—There is no fear in love; but perfect love casteth out fear: because fear hath torment. He that feareth is not made perfect in love.

PERSONAL REFLECTION:

Question: Do you have a habit of being critical and judgmental toward people? Think of ways that this pattern of thinking could be affecting you emotionally.

9

Adversaries and trials are strategically designed for parts of our lives with purpose to produce growth and maturity. Trying to escape through one door and find refuge in a room you choose for yourself will only lead to a bigger trial that you are not prepared to tackle.

In the book of Genesis, chapter 15, God promised Abraham an heir; a child; a seed. God made this promise to Abraham in their intimate time of communion. In chapter 16 of the book of Genesis, Abraham was convinced by his wife's logical account of their situation. "Logically, we do not have a child of our own and we have been waiting for a long time. Just take Hagar, our maid, and allow our seed to be born through her." Great idea, but this was not God's plan. Abraham listened to his wife and Hagar gave birth to Ishmael. This plan was originally Sarah's idea; why was she then so frustrated and unsettled with the result? Her idea brought forth contempt, disarray, and warring, to this very day.

When God presents us with a challenge, it is meant to build our faith and character. When we try to avoid challenges, our journey becomes difficult because the resources needed to overcome the trial will only be found in our victory over our assigned test. The test and resources are in the door we chose to avoid; we have to go back, we skipped a step. When we do not yield to God's plan, we will experience depression, hopelessness, and anxiety because there is only peace when we are assured of His leading in our lives. We as mortal beings are aware of our limitations, and there is no way that we can have confidence in ourselves and expect to win. We know that we cannot win, but our God can.

Abraham's journey to his ultimate purpose in God did not have to yield such disorder and division. However, he chose a course that seemed easier and allowed the voice of another who was not part of his intimate time with the Lord to be louder than his Father's voice. He believed in the rationale rather than the miracle. I thank God that He is a God of mercy. God's purpose was still fulfilled. The Lord told Abraham again in Genesis 17:19, just in case he did not hear God the first time, "And God said, Sarah thy wife shall bear thee a son indeed; and thou shalt call his name Isaac: and I will establish my covenant with him for an everlasting covenant, and with his seed after him."

God was allowing faith to be birthed in Abraham. The course may be difficult, but it will bring forth a profitable reward in the end. We at times experience depression when we are hoping for things that seem to be delayed. And rightly so, according to Proverbs 13:12—"Hope deferred maketh the heart sick: but when the desire cometh, it is a tree of life." However, the skill is to change our perspective of our waiting season and glean the best from it. Ask ourselves, "What is God birthing in me to prepare me for that which I am waiting for?" God was birthing faith in Abraham. What is He birthing in you?

Our thought patterns around our situation have to line up with God's Word and that which He reveals to us in the Spirit. God's Word is meant to encourage us throughout our journey and give us hope. If we think that our heavenly Father does not care for us and has destructive thoughts toward us, then yes, our situations will feel unbearable and cause much depression. But if we know that our God has good thoughts toward us and plans to prosper us and give us an expected end, we would have boldness as Abraham had when he was challenged to offer up his son Isaac as a sacrifice. Abraham knew the kind of God he served and was not moved by anxiety; he had pure trust and hope in God. God did not fail Abraham and He will not fail us. As God provided a sacrifice for Abraham, a ram in place of his son Isaac, God will provide a way of escape for us.

Spiritual Food for Thought:

Hebrews 11:1—Now faith is the substance of things hoped for, the evidence of things not seen.

PERSONAL REFLECTION:

Question: What challenges are you facing currently? How has your view of your challenges influenced your ability to cope with your challenges?

10

Your season of waiting is to build patience. The longer it takes for you to acquire this virtue, the longer it will take for you to enter your place of promise.

I love the Word of God, both Old and New Testament. But I am more fascinated with the Old Testament because I really see God fully through His works with the children of Israel. In the book of Exodus, God promised the children of Israel that He would take them to the Promised Land. A journey that was supposed to only take eleven days took forty years; not one or two years, but forty. Wow! God was not limited in His ability to bring them into the land flowing with milk and honey; rather, the children of Israel's hearts were not ready to enter in.

What was it about their hearts that caused a delay in their blessing? They had ungratefulness, they were full of fear, and idolatry was their go-to when God did not work fast enough. Despite the miracles that God performed for the Israelites to make them believe that He was with them, they still doubted. God could have taken the children of Israel by the way of the Philistines, but He was mindful of their weakness and took them through the wilderness to prevent them from being discouraged by war. God had their best interest in mind and was not against them, yet because of their own hearts, their perception of God and His plan for them was tainted.

I remember when I graduated with my bachelor's degree from Liberty University in Lynchburg, Virginia, I was anxious to find a good-paying, well-established job. Before graduating, I started praying and fasting, and I was confident that God had something special just for me. Well, the applications started, the interviews came, and no offers. For a year I went through a period of depression and anxiety; my expectations did not meet my reality. It was deeper than not finding employment, it was my attitude in the process. Within that year, I became bitter, angry, rude, and I was in a state of defeat. God had to show me what was really in my heart. I am going to go a bit deeper. When He did show up and gave me a full-time position, it was not what I was hoping for. He started me off as a substitute teacher for pre-kindergarten at the one and only Christian Heritage Academy, then to a teacher's assistant position. I stayed there for three years until I was able to work out my heart issue. I could not go on to my next stage with all the things that were in my heart. But through it all, God's purpose was still being fulfilled. Those times of learning and growth are still for Him. Before leaving Christian Heritage Academy and moving into what I call my "career calling," I met my husband and it is all history from there.

At times we are focused on acquiring and receiving what we are seeking God for, and that is not the place where God wants our thoughts to be. God actually wants us to focus on the part of us that He is cultivating. When we are constantly fixed on the process and not so much the end result, we will experience less anxiety. I oftentimes challenge my patients who experience severe anxiety around something they are waiting for or rushing to accomplish with the questions: What is the rush? What are you missing in the process of rushing? What part of you in your pattern of rushing are you not valuing or perfecting that will be needed when you finally accomplish your goal? I challenge myself with these questions when I become anxious about a process. I find comfort in the thought pattern that if God has not presented it to me yet, I am just not ready. I am aware of my maladaptive thought patterns that lead to anxiety and quickly change my thoughts and perception of my situations, which always leads to a more peaceful emotion.

Spiritual Food for Thought:

Job 14:14—If a man die, shall he live again? all the days of my appointed time will I wait, till my change come.

PERSONAL REFLECTION:

Question: What promise/promises are you waiting to come to pass in your life? What parts of your character is God building through your process of waiting?

11

Without the right perspective, you are vulnerable to illusions. Change your position and the right perspective will follow.

My understanding of perspectives changed when I learned about the *Ames room*. The Ames room was created by Adelbert Ames Jr., an American ophthalmologist. In 1946, the first Ames room was built to reflect the process of distorted perception as a result of one's position. The Ames room looks like a normal rectangular shape when it is viewed from the front, but in actuality, it is trapezoidal. The walls from the front appear to be parallel, but they are not; they are slanted. Being inside the room will taint your perspective. To add even more of an illusion, checkered floors were added and rectangular windows were added to the back wall.

The purpose of the Ames room is to clearly understand the significant role that past experiences play in individuals' current, supposed world. How are you viewing the situations around you? This topic brings me to the story of David and his perception of Goliath. David had previous experiences of defeating a lion and a bear. First Samuel 17:34–36 says, "And David said unto Saul, Thy servant kept his father's sheep, and there came a lion, and a bear, and took a lamb out of the flock: And I went out after him, and smote him, and delivered it out of his mouth: and when he arose against me, I caught him by his beard, and smote him, and slew him. Thy servant slew both the lion and the bear: and this uncircumcised Philistine shall be as one of them, seeing he hath defied the armies of the living God." David's perception was significantly different from the men in Saul's army as well as his brothers because of his past circumstances where he first handily experienced the victory of God. His faith was stronger and his confidence was much higher. If David did not have the challenge of overtaking a bear and a lion, his faith may not have been so strong and as a youth he may not have been as confident as he was to defeat a giant.

Challenges in your life are necessary, and you have to embrace them as they are your mode of transportation to the next level; they lead to your elevation. My mother-in-law texted me a powerful encouraging word one day, and she said, "Pass the tests today, if not those hurdles will keep coming until you successfully jump over all." My mother would always encourage me with these same words in my youthful days, and as a result, I began to perceive my challenges as opportunities. But there is an adversary that we encounter daily who does not want to see us overcome our challenges; he is intimidated by our destiny. And so, he creates Ames rooms in our minds and distorts our perception. He influences our thinking by telling us that our challenges are going to break us or that God is against us and that is why we are going through difficulties in our lives. As a result of the enemy's lies and our distorted perception, we become downcast, hopeless, and depressed. Gain the right perception by positioning yourself in God's Word. Isaiah 54:17 says, "'No weapon formed against you shall prosper, And every tongue which rises against you in judgment you shall condemn. This is the heritage of the servants of the Lord, And their righteousness is from Me,' Says the Lord" (NKJV).

When you are listening to the voice of God, you will always hear life and hope. Judge whose voice you are listening to by whether the result is life or death. God has come that we may have life; He is not a God of death. Anytime you see or hear death, know that you are in the wrong position, thus leading to the wrong perception. Remain in the Spirit and you will always have life.

Spiritual Food for Thought:

John 10:10—The thief cometh not, but for to steal, and to kill, and to destroy: I am come that they might have life, and that they might have it more abundantly.

PERSONAL REFLECTION:

Question: Have you taken time to reflect on your perspectives? If you were to challenge yourself by judging your perspectives, what can you say about how they have skewed your vision of your challenges and led to unwelcome feelings?

12

As healthy food is nourishment for the body, so healthy thoughts are nourishment for the heart and soul.

Eating healthy has great pathological benefits on the body. According to WebMD, when we have a nourishing, balanced diet daily, with the right amount of vitamins, minerals, and nutrients, will help you feel great and will also increase your level of energy. Eating the right kinds of foods with variation daily can also help to reduce stress. A great prevention to heart disease, high blood pressure, type 2 diabetes, and some cases of cancer is a well-balanced, healthy diet.

Uniquely, there are some types of healthy foods that target parts of the body they resemble. Here are a couple: Carrots, when viewed crosswise, resemble the eye, and you will notice a radiating pattern of lines like those in your pupil and iris. It is proven that carrots help to promote healthy eyes. With their element of beta-carotene and antioxidants, carrots are known to decrease the likelihood of macular degeneration. According to Dr. Sasson Moulavi, macular degeneration is the leading cause of vision loss in older adults. Another food that targets the part of the body it resembles is celery. Celery is long and lean like our bones. Celery provides our bones with silicon, giving them strength. A unique fact, according to *Woman's Day*, is that bones are twenty-three percent sodium, just like celery.

Now, let's take a look at the benefits of healthy thinking. According to Kendra Cherry, our thoughts and feelings are significantly instrumental in influencing our behaviors. An example that was used by Kendra

Cherry was that if a person constantly thinks about plane crashes, runway accidents, or other air catastrophes, they may avoid air travel. In comparison, if we think of ourselves as failures, or destined for failure, we will not take the necessary steps to progress or achieve great things; we will definitely experience stagnancy.

At some point in life we experience defeating thoughts and struggle with unhealthy thinking patterns. We have encounters with unhealthy thoughts, but that does not mean we have to remain consistent in that way of thinking to the point that it becomes a pattern. If we say that we want to eat healthier because we become aware of the benefits of better eating habits, it does not mean that we will actually change; we will not change just by being aware. Awareness is the first step and after awareness, we then have to make a step toward change. After change is made, we then have to establish a habit, pattern, and motivation to keep us on our journey to eating better. This same concept applies to healthy thinking.

Cognitive behavioral therapy is an intervention/psychotherapeutic treatment model that challenges individuals to identify destructive thoughts in order to exhibit better behaviors. Cognitive behavioral therapy is most commonly used as an intervention for phobias, addictions, depression, and anxiety; all of these conditions are associated with maladaptive thought processes. The goal of cognitive behavioral therapy is to change undesirable behavior patterns.

Here is the taboo question: Do Christians have patterns of thinking that are maladaptive? Absolutely. And some of us are living in depression, anxiety, and addiction to behaviors or unhealthy engagements that deprives us of spiritual growth and leaves us spiritually weak and stagnant in our walk with the Lord. Deliverance needs to happen in the mind. Once we are aware and honest with ourselves, we can begin the journey to mental healing.

Spiritual Food for Thought:

Romans 12:2—And be not conformed to this world: but be ye transformed by the renewing of your mind, that ye may prove what is that good, and acceptable, and perfect, will of God.

PERSONAL REFLECTION:

Question: Have you been struggling with any undesirable feelings that you just cannot shake (i.e., depression, anxiety, jealousy)? What thought patterns can you identify that have led to the particular feeling/feelings you identified?

The good things that you do are seeds for your harvest. So are the evil things that you do; be sure to sow seeds of goodness.

What harvest do you want to reap? Everyone has a season of blessings, and the extent of your blessing is dependent on how you respond to another person's season. Your time is coming; rejoice with your brother as you would want others to also rejoice with you.

The Word of God speaks about jealousy and covetousness, which means that it is very much present in the hearts of individuals. First Corinthians 3:2–3 says, "I have fed you with milk, and not with meat: for hitherto ye were not able to bear it, neither yet now are ye able. For ye are yet carnal: for whereas there is among you envying, and strife, and divisions, are ye not carnal, and walk as men?" I sat with a patient who I treated a few years ago and spoke with her about her relationship with her family members. When she mentioned her younger sister, her top lip flared for less than a second. With the training that I have in micro facial expression, I was able to point out her reaction and challenged her to talk about what that meant. She expressed that her sister is younger than her and was doing so much better than her and she hated it. How many of us can identify with this dynamic and/or this feeling?

It is not natural to accept someone being better than us, and it is even harder when it is a family member, or better yet, our sibling. But here is something to think about: if we were the person succeeding or if we had achieved a great accomplishment, how would we want others to respond to our success and accomplishments? When God decides that it is our turn and He elevates us, what kind of support and affirmation would we want from those around us? If we do not affirm and support those we had the opportunity to, there will be periods in our lives wherein that same energy will come back to us. I am not saying that as individuals, we will not have feelings of jealousy and covetousness, but we should not water those feelings further with our reoccurring thoughts. Instead, water them with the Word of God to combat our thoughts. God wants us to be responsible and aware enough to manage it.

I know that for some of us, we do not play around when it comes to our finances. When we realize that our checkbook roster is getting out of control because we have been too relaxed with managing our bills, we have that light bulb moment; we immediately change our habits. For some of us, it requires cutting back on our spending and re-budgeting, and for others it may be to just organize and record our spending better. Whatever the circumstance may be, when we have a family that is dependent on us to make responsible decisions, we make sure that we get it done. Well, the same is true when it comes to our spiritual walk. God has charged us with the responsibility to check things in our lives that have the potential to get out of control. Part of God's expectation for us is treating those in our lives without jealousy, which, if left unchecked, can lead to contempt.

When we think about jealousy, it is another way of telling God that He is not fair, and this can greatly influence our perception of God and life. Many people experience severe depression because they are not happy with their life due to the comparison with another person's life. When contentment is not present, hope is diminished and gratitude is far from our hearts. God wants to relieve us of this pain by giving us the right mind-frame. However, we have to be willing to accept it. We accept relief by first acknowledging our thinking pattern of jealousy and being aware of how this feeling has led to contempt. We then continue our journey by conforming our thoughts to God's Word about how we should relate to those around us. Matthew 22:37–39 says, "And he said to him, 'You shall love the Lord your God with all your heart and with all your soul and with all your mind. This is the great and first commandment. And a second is like it: You shall love your neighbor as yourself'" (ESV).

I live my life with the mantra, "be the person you want others to be to you or treat others the way you would like to be treated." Do I experience great reassurance and respectful treatment from people all the time? No, I do not, but I have assurance through Luke 6:31, "And as ye would that men should do to you, do ye also to them likewise." God will allow good treatment to come my way, but woe to those who were the agent of wrongdoing or mistreatment. I challenge you to be the person who does good, wishes others well, and models respect and love for the next generation. The more of *you* there are, the better this world will be.

Spiritual Food for Thought:

> **Romans 12:15**—Rejoice with them that do rejoice, and weep with them that weep.

PERSONAL REFLECTION:

Question: Is there any seed of jealousy or covetousness in your life that has led to discord with someone in your life? Do you have a pattern of comparing your life to others' lives?

Love is a very potent weapon that is seldom used. I will not be a product of my enemy's actions toward me.

How hard is it to love someone who you, in fact, know does not like you, much less love you? Very hard. My husband often says that it is outside of our nature as human beings to love our enemy, and that is why we need to remain in the Spirit in order to accomplish this task, and that is also the reason why we have to work so hard at it. In retrospect, I've noticed that great levels of elevation occurred when I was able to overcome feelings of hurt and resentment as a result of someone's increased effort to mistreat me. A mindfulness technique that I oftentimes practice, because it works well for me, is compassion. I think of the love that the Lord has for us that drew Him to the cross. When I allow my mind to go in this direction, my level of mercy and compassion for my enemies increases.

Compassion is exercised when we are thoughtful of others' vulnerability. I think to myself, *If you knew to do better, you would, and because you are struggling with doing what is right, I feel for you.* When I think along these lines when it comes to my enemies, I automatically change my feelings from resentment to empathy. We are all on the path to being better people, and what may be my strengths just may be your weakness and vice versa. I am then compelled to intercede and pray for you rather than fight the internal battle of hate and contempt.

When we exercise compassion for ourselves and others, does that mean we will not be challenged with thoughts of retaliation, isolation, and separation? Yes, we will. Allow me to be a little transparent. I can say that for years I struggled with isolating myself from people who I perceived were an emotional threat and who have done things to hurt me. Especially when I knew that it was intentional. I would always think that it is one thing to hurt me accidentally, meaning that you were not aware that a particular thing offended me. But it is another thing when you actually go out of your way to hurt me emotionally. Isolating to me looked like "cutting people off." It was very easy for me to do. Then I realized how damaging that was to my calling and purpose in Christ.

The thought of being able to reach people and be that example by modeling and showing others the right way is not possible if I am separated from them. How can God be glorified from acts of division and separation? I was also challenged with thoughts of what would happen to my life if God retaliates, isolates, and separates from me? Where would my hope come from? With that thought, I am propelled to open the lines of hope and forgiveness for myself by extending hope and forgiveness to others. Do I only sin on accident or are there times when I sin intentionally, with my eyes wide open? Yes, there are, and God still extends mercy to me and to you.

Romans 5:8 says, "But God demonstrates his own love for us in this: While we were still sinners, Christ died for us" (NIV). Christ gave of Himself as a way to show us how much He loves us. When we were sinners, we were enemies to God. The way God loved us when we were His enemies is the same way He expects us to love those who have made us their enemies, in order to win them and point them in the right direction: the way to heaven. The only way we will make it to heaven is through the four-letter word LOVE. Loving others is not a negotiation, it is a requirement; it is a command.

Spiritual Food for Thought:

Luke 6:27-28—But to you who are listening I say: Love your enemies, do good to those who hate you, bless those who curse you, pray for those who mistreat you. (NIV)

PERSONAL REFLECTION:

Question: In what part of your life are you struggling with loving others? On a scale of one to ten, with one being very little and ten being very often, how often do you exercise compassion daily?

15

Forgiveness is a power tool, as it frees the heart of the forgiver and lightens the weight of the one in need of forgiveness.

The lack of forgiveness is the cause of many sicknesses as well as struggles with anxiety and anger. We are not physically and mentally built to carry loads of unforgiveness and fear. Fear comes from the presence of hopelessness and the need to control. When we give someone hope by offering forgiveness, we in return open doors of hope for ourselves. Truth is, you feel the weight because you're not only carrying another person's sin; you are also carrying your own sins. If you do not forgive others of their trespass toward you, God will not forgive your trespass toward Him. Let go and allow God to work it out; you are not in control.

Have you ever thought of the wrong that you do to another person as sin against God? Maybe if we were aware of the fact that what we do to another person is actually not just an act to that person but an act to God, then we would consider our behaviors more. Matthew 25:34–40 says, "Then shall the King say unto them on his right hand, Come, ye blessed of my Father, inherit the kingdom prepared for you from the foundation of the world: For I was an hungred, and ye gave me meat: I was thirsty, and ye gave me drink: I was a stranger, and ye took me in: Naked, and ye clothed me: I was sick, and ye visited me: I was in prison, and ye came unto me. Then shall the righteous answer him, saying, Lord, when saw we thee an hungred, and fed thee? or thirsty, and gave thee drink? When saw we thee a stranger, and took thee in? or naked, and clothed thee? Or when saw we thee sick, or in prison, and came unto thee? And the King shall answer and say unto them, Verily I say unto you, Inasmuch as ye have done it unto one of the least of these my brethren, ye have done it unto me."

I remember an injury that I sustained to my right foot in 2016. There was a broken tooth of a comb on my bathroom floor that I stepped on accidentally. I took the piece out of my foot but experienced unbearable pain for months in the same spot. I thought that the area was badly bruised. After weeks of what should have resulted in healing of the area, I went to the emergency room, but the doctor had no solution for me. I was told that it was a lesion that just needed time to heal.

I had just started a new job at the Jewish Board of Family and Children's Services at the time and had to attend weeks of training. The training site was in Manhattan and I had to walk at least four long blocks to get to the site after getting off the train; no buses ran in that direction. Through this entire ordeal, my heart was heavy with a sister who I worshipped with at the time. One day after church, the Lord started working on my heart around forgiveness and I genuinely forgave the sister who I resented. We had such warm and genuine fellowship with each other, and I spent most of the evening talking and connecting with her. That very same night when I got home, I sat at the side of my bed, talking to my mother about my forgiveness experience and how good it felt. In that moment, I felt a sensation in my right foot, and when I looked at the bottom of my foot, a piece of the tooth of the comb that I stepped on months prior was coming out of my foot in the area where I was having unbearable pain. This is the result of forgiveness!

Since I had this experience, I have been so quick to let go of offense, bitterness, unforgiveness, or any feeling that will delay healing and blessings from flowing my way. Luckily, I was able to see what was stuck in my foot, but there are some spiritual healings and blessings that are delayed simply because we will not forgive. Forgive easily and your blessings will follow. The longer it takes you to forgive, the longer it will take for you to receive that which you have been hoping for.

Spiritual Food for Thought:

Mark 11:25—And when ye stand praying, forgive, if ye have ought against any: that your Father also which is in heaven may forgive you your trespasses.

PERSONAL REFLECTION:

Question: Have you been struggling with resistance to forgive? Are you aware of the results of your unwillingness to forgive?

16

Hands stretched up are a sign of surrender to God. When we surrender to God, we are guaranteed to receive victory.

Where there is a lack of breakthrough in our life, there is a lack of full surrender. Not just one hand up, but full surrender requires both hands. There are parts of us we may be aware of that are unproductive and very difficult to change or surrender. Many times, we are aware of dysfunctions in our lives personally or in our lives as a family that have been part of us for so long that they have become comfortable to live with. But we are not mindful of how these dysfunctional patterns have contributed to our anxiety, depression, and even overall unhappiness; this state of being has become normal to us. When we get to that point of being so completely overwhelmed that we have a moment of complete mental exhaustion or, as some may call it, a mental breakdown, this could be God's way of saying, "I want to move you from being dysfunctional to functional." Failure has become a normal state for you, poverty has become normal, lack of power and influence has become normal, and even sin has become the norm.

For some of us, as children we were taught that continuous victory was not possible; we only experienced failure and defeat. However, God has called His people to surrender defeating mindsets to Him. Yes, it is very difficult to think and function at a higher level than we are taught as children, and that is why studying God's Word and establishing godly accountability is very important. Proverbs 27:17 says, "Iron sharpeneth iron; so a man sharpeneth the countenance of his friend."

In Exodus 17:10–13, we see that Moses needed both of his hands raised in order to continue to receive victory for Israel. Moses was surrendered to God and stood as a representative for Israel. As a result of Israel's surrender to God, they were victorious. We get weary at times as Moses did and need help or assistance on our journey. In times of exhaustion, we should pray for God to send us an Aaron and a Hur to hold us up in times of weakness and hold us accountable around our defeating thoughts and actions.

Accountability is not a suggested ingredient, it's a necessity. Accountability provides us with encouragement and a new perspective on our situations. The danger of depending on just ourselves for guidance is that our thoughts and views are not always right; at times, they are skewed and subjective. Through talking, we discover a lot about ourselves. Having people who are able to point our thoughts in the right direction when they take a wrong turn can save us time and unnecessary distress.

Let's take a quick look at commuting with a Global Positioning System (GPS). The purpose of a GPS is to direct us to our desired destination, and we can, for the sake of this metaphor, call the GPS our accountability partner. If we make a wrong turn, either the GPS signals us to reroute or it will calculate an alternative option for our commute. The great thing about a GPS is that it points out our wrong turn right away so that we can correct it; this saves us time and distress. Thank God for Roger L. Easton and for his expertise around some engineering applications used to develop the GPS. Full surrender resembles our actions in listening to the GPS say, "Re-routing, turn left," and we immediately turn left. We are set on the right track when we listen and take heed, when we fully surrender.

I remember in the days before 1995 when traveling with my parents, we relied on printing out directions online and still missed several turns and exits. I remember stopping at gas stations to find out how to get back on the right track after being on the wrong path for too long. Our expected time of arrival would be three o'clock p.m., but we would not reach our destination until six p.m. simply because of one wrong turn. So, too, in our lives, when we've missed our path or are heading down an unproductive path of destruction in life, we need people to point it out to us, and in humility we should just change and get back on the right path. We need to listen to our GPS. We need to surrender.

When we have an Aaron and a Hur in our lives, cherish them and honor them; they will save us time and distress. We will find victory when we surrender completely and allow God to direct our path. When we missed our exits, in my experience with traveling with my parents, it would lead to huge arguments, and by the time we reached our destination, no one would want to stay because everyone was in a bad mood. Full surrender does not lead to a bad mood, but it is rather a relief.

God's plan for our lives is not to be in a defeating, unproductive position. God wants us to surrender our lives completely to Him so He can reveal His elevated thoughts of us, to us. God has called us to be conquerors, leaders, and overcomers. God wants us to dream and be aware of what our position in Him looks like. However, if we are not surrendering our lives completely to Him, we will not see the whole picture. We will see part, but not the whole. When we surrender, we relinquish control to God, and as a result, we will notice that our level of anxieties will decrease. God's voice may come from an Aaron in our lives or a Hur. However the Lord chooses to speak, all we have to do is listen. Where there is a lack of growth, there is a lack of complete and total surrender.

Spiritual Food for Thought:

James 4:7—Submit yourselves, then, to God. Resist the devil, and he will flee from you. (NIV)

PERSONAL REFLECTION:

Question: What part of your life are you struggling with fully surrendering to God? Who are the Aarons and Hurs in your life?

17

I am the head and not the tail. I am above and not beneath. I am more than a conqueror through Christ Jesus. I can do all things through Christ who gives me strength.

Research shows that people perceive interactions with others differently based on their personality. For example, an introverted person views their interactions with people more negatively because they feel judged based on their own insecurities. People who are extroverts, on the other hand, are more confident in their interactions with others and tend to view their conversations more positively; they also receive energy from their back-and-forth connections and relationships. Introverts generally feel drained of their energy after socializing. Does this mean that being an introvert is a bad personality trait and being an extrovert is good? Not necessarily, but it does, however, require more mental discipline for an introverted person to think more confidently and combat the thoughts that they are bombarded with when interacting. The purpose, assignment, and life course of an introverted person may be completely different because God knows what He has created that person for and what he or she can handle, but whatever that assignment is, it is still going to require confidence and boldness.

How do we become confident and bold if it is not a part of our nature? Great question. Let's look at Moses again. When God told Moses to go to Pharaoh and tell him to let His people go, how did Moses respond? According to Exodus 3:11, Moses said, "Who am I, that I should go unto Pharaoh, and that I should bring forth the children of

Israel out of Egypt?" Moses had no confidence in himself; he thought of his weaknesses. In Exodus 4:10, Moses says, "O my Lord, I am not eloquent, neither heretofore, nor since thou hast spoken unto thy servant: but I am slow of speech, and of a slow tongue." We should not rely on our strengths to accomplish our destined purpose, but rather we should rely on the Lord: His confidence, His abilities, His wisdom, and His strength. Allow Him to do the work through us and we will always have victory. When God is on the scene, the impossible happens.

What is the danger of relying on self? It leads to pride. We see in Daniel 4:30–32 Nebuchadnezzar testifies of how God humbled him. He says in verse 30, "Is not this great Babylon, that I have built for the house of the kingdom by the might of my power, and for the honour of my majesty? While the word was in the king's mouth, there fell a voice from heaven, saying, O king Nebuchadnezzar, to thee it is spoken; The kingdom is departed from thee. And they shall drive thee from men, and thy dwelling shall be with the beasts of the field: they shall make thee to eat grass as oxen, and seven times shall pass over thee, until thou know that the most High ruleth in the kingdom of men, and giveth it to whomsoever he will." When we rely on ourselves, we take God out of the picture and failure is inevitable. When we experience failure, it is normal to experience a decrease in confidence.

When we position ourselves in God and allow Him to direct the course of our lives, we will definitely have jaw-dropping experiences with Him. God wants us to have a personal walk with Him and learn of His qualities firsthand. The more we know of who He is, the more we will know about who we are. As believers of God, we cannot define ourselves outside of Him. Through my experiences with God, I have been able to build confidence to say boldly that I am the head and I am not the tail. My heavenly Father is the ruler of the universe. My heavenly Father created the heavens and the earth. My heavenly Father parted the Red Sea for the children of Israel. With knowing these parts of God, I have had great expectations in my journey: that God will rule over my situations, He will create great paths for me and will part barriers in my way. And He has done all mentioned and more. When we are defined in God, there is no "I don't know what my purpose is" or "I do not know who I am." Being unclear in who we are and what we were created for leads to a disposition of hopelessness, which leads to depression. Define yourself in God and know with surety that He has created you for greatness.

Spiritual Food for Thought:

Colossians 2:10—And ye are complete in him, which is the head of all principality and power.

PERSONAL REFLECTION:

Question: What have been your experiences with God that increase your level of confidence and hope? What parts of confidence do you lack due to your reliance on self?

18

Do you think of yourself more highly than you ought to? What is the danger in this way of thinking? Moreover, what kind of road are you creating to being the most effective person because of these thoughts?

Romans 12:3 says, "For I say, through the grace given unto me, to every man that is among you, not to think of himself more highly than he ought to think; but to think soberly, according as God hath dealt to every man the measure of faith." When we put expectations on ourselves that are higher than God has allowed us, we set ourselves up for failures, which also affect our emotions and self-confidence. When we create unrealistic goals for ourselves that do not line up with God's vision and we fail, we experience low self-esteem, and some individuals even blame God.

As we have already seen, Nebuchadnezzar gloried in his accomplishment of building Babylon. He said, "Is not this great Babylon, that I have built for the house of the kingdom by the might of my power, and for the honour of my majesty?" Nebuchadnezzar did not realize that he could only do as much and go as far as God allowed him. We at times forget how limited we are. If we are skilled, gifted, or advanced in any area of life, it's because God allowed it, not because of our greatness, but simply because of His excellence. God's expectation for us is to dream and allow Him to bring it to pass; be sure to give Him the glory in the end. Ultimately, our gifts and our talents are in line with His purpose and plan for our assignment in life.

Our thoughts for self have to line up with God's thoughts and His timing. God expects us to dream and aspire, but be sure to dream in sync with Him. Your thoughts may be on that goal that you have set and you may say to yourself, "I am going to do this in five to six months because I know God wants me to succeed." However, in actuality, God may want you working on a different project that will also yield success or He may want you to pursue that particular ambition right away rather than wait five to six months. The point is, we have to be sure that we consult with God and His thoughts for our lives. Jeremiah 29:11 says, "For I know the thoughts that I think toward you, saith the Lord, thoughts of peace, and not of evil, to give you an expected end." Notice that God has thoughts. At times, we give God our thoughts and want Him to bless them. However, what God wants is for us to seek Him to learn His thoughts. When we seek God first, we can easily avoid unproductive patterns that lead to constant failure and disappointment.

I recall a message by T. D. Jakes wherein he talked about reading product manuals prior to using the products. He stated that at times, we avoid reading the manual and when we experience a malfunction we go back to the first step we skipped to correct the issue, when the issue could have probably been avoided if we just read the manual first. More time is used to correct the process that went wrong. If we just consult with God about His plans for our life, we could avoid a lot of problems and setbacks. God's process and timing is perfect, and He will give you the instructions that will yield positive results.

Once we are coordinated with God's timing and agenda, sustaining success or change is inevitable. God gives us good ideas and strategies to be successful in whatever we do. If we are not seeking Him, however, we will not gain light of those good ideas and strategies. Wisdom is not relying on our own ability, but rather it is trusting only in God. Our situation may not be very promising in reality, but with God's supernatural power it will work out in our favor. Vice versa, our situation may look very promising without consulting with God but will eventually collapse because we relied on ourselves. If we do something over and over and do not get the right results, it is best that we try something different. If we've been relying on self and have been disappointed every time, it is best that we try Jesus and rely on Him. We will be guaranteed favorable results.

Spiritual Food for Thought:

Proverbs 3:6—In all thy ways acknowledge him, and he shall direct thy paths.

PERSONAL REFLECTION:

Question: What thinking patterns of self-glory can you identify? How can you challenge yourself around lining up your thoughts with God's Word?

19

Good character will open doors for you that bad character closes. Change your character and experience a change in your life.

One of my favorite Old Testament accounts is that of Esther. We live in a world where we are taught that in order to be counted as the elite, to be among those of high degree, or to acquire the best in life, you have to come from a "well-off" family, carry a significant family name, or just know the right people. My mother used to say and still does say, "Money rubs with money." Meaning, if you have money, you connect and associate with other people of the same financial status to increase your chances of marrying or partnering with people just like you. You also have a sense of comfort in being around people like you—wealthy people. What I love about my God is that He defies these systems and operates completely opposite of these systems. In the book of Esther, chapter 2, we learn that Esther was an orphan; she did not have a father or a mother and was being cared for by her cousin, Mordecai. Esther could have been a bitter person when she saw other girls who had their parents to care for them, but instead, she was content with her cousin and respected him greatly.

When we look in Esther chapter 1, we see the complete opposite attitude of Vashti, King Ahasuerus's wife, the queen. The Word of God says that Vashti was very beautiful to look at and when King Ahasuerus called for her during his feast time, she refused him. God created an opportunity to place the "have nots" with the haves; not because of economic status, but simply because He is a strategic God and is very attracted to the right attitude and character. Due to Vashti's attitude and act of dishonor to the king, she lost her position as queen, and in the process, Esther inherited her position. Look at God! Esther had the right attitude, which launched her to her position. Vashti lacked the gratitude that Esther had.

If your attitude and character is flawed, the questions that I would ask are, what are your thoughts about your life and your particular situations? Is gratitude present? There is such power in having a heart of gratitude. In a mindfulness training I attended, the instructor gave an amazing suggestion on how to incorporate gratitude in our day. As trainees, we were challenged to think of a time when we had a really bad migraine headache or back pain. When we are in the predicament, all we can think of is how great it would be if we just did not have the pain or how pleasant it would feel if the pain just went away. As we thought of the pain and the fact that we were not feeling the pain in that moment, gratitude was in the room. If we wake up every morning and think about a predicament that was devastating that we are not experiencing in that moment, we will be motivated to be grateful and our attitudes will become attractive to God, which will lead us into great opportunities.

It does not matter how bad your situation may be, there is something to be grateful for; if it's even the absence of that excruciating headache you had once in your life that you do not have now, be thankful just for that! Thankfulness can create a more positive attitude and create the space for a better mood. Having a moody day? Find something to give thanks for. Create the space in your mind to think of things that are going well. Even if it is one thing, magnify that one thing and be thankful.

Spiritual Food for Thought:

First Thessalonians 5:18—In every thing give thanks: for this is the will of God in Christ Jesus concerning you.

PERSONAL REFLECTION:

Question: What are some negative attitudes that you can identify in your life? How has your attitude affected your mood and view of your life?

20

God has given us all that we need to live our best life. In order to value our best, we need to encounter our worst at some point in our life trajectory.

I remember when I gave my life to the Lord, I wanted to do everything right. My thought around doing everything right was that nothing in my life would go wrong. It was smooth sailing here on out and I was going to make it to the top because my God is on top. Things worked well for me in the beginning, but then the real process started: the process of growth and being stretched. As I began to mature in my walk of life and in God, I realized that when elevation is about to happen, there is a challenge—a specific circumstance that I had to overcome in order to make it to the next level.

Overcoming a challenge in order to make it to the next level in life reminds me of playing video games. I am not an expert on video games, but when I was younger, I enjoyed playing Super Mario Bros. On level one, I was a guru, but as I progressed in the game, the challenges became harder and harder. There was this specific part that I just could not master and there was no moving on from there. This is identical to our walk of life and our growth in the Lord. We must go through levels of mastering a particular area in life in order to move on to a greater level.

Jesus Christ Himself had to go through preparation and challenges to make it to the next level of His purpose. Before Christ went to the cross, He had to go through a time of testing to make sure that He was ready for the journey of giving His life for us. His walk was also not self-centered, but it was rather focused on giving of Himself so others can live. Any endeavor that is self-centered is not in line with God, and He is not obligated to shine on that effort. But when we submit ourselves to God, He will show us the way that we should go and we will be guaranteed to make it through victoriously. With God, there is losing in order to gain. When we make movements of our own accord, we will lose. We may gain for a while, but it will not profit much good in the end. Mark 8:34 says, "And when he had called the people unto him with his disciples also, he said unto them, Whosoever will come after me, let him deny himself, and take up his cross, and follow me." Be encouraged and know that there are great rewards in following wholeheartedly after Christ.

When we are not willing to go through times of testing and character building in our valley, we will not be able to make it to the mountain. God is not interested in us "making it"; He is more interested in how we make it. At times we get so focused on the goal that we lose sight of the process. Many of us encounter anxiety because we are so focused on accomplishing. However, if we take time to enjoy the journey and the process of the journey, we will realize the importance in our growth and experience less anxiety. The building of our character does not happen in our accomplishment, it occurs in the process to our accomplishment. If we appreciate our challenging days, God will be able to sustain our good days.

I've mentioned David a lot throughout this devotional because there are so many valuable parts of him that we can learn from. Even though David loved the Lord, he was still flawed in character as we all are. When David became king and sinned against God by sleeping with Uriah's wife, we can see throughout the book of Psalms his focus was on the inner him that needed to be fixed: his character. God had to break David in order to fix him; tear him down in order to build him up again. David's prayer became prayers of focus on the inner him.

Psalm 139:23–24 says, "Search me, O God, and know my heart: try me, and know my thoughts: And see if there be any wicked way in me, and lead me in the way everlasting." Our God is concerned and overwhelmed by the state of our souls. The Lord knows the importance of being in right standing with Him and uses valley experiences to get us to that state. You will experience peace and hope with God working on you rather than despair and loss with Him being far from you. When we are aware of this process, we will value the bad days more and thank God for them.

Spiritual Food for Thought:

Mark 8:36—For what shall it profit a man, if he shall gain the whole world, and lose his own soul?

PERSONAL REFLECTION:

Question: Reflect back on some challenging days you've experienced or are experiencing. What lessons did you or are you learning and what part of your character has been or is being cultivated?

In order to enter in the land of promise, we must be prepared. Every situation we face, whether good or bad, is just preparation.

Jesus Christ said in John 14 that He has gone to prepare a place for us, with many mansions. Everything requires preparation; even the creator of this universe needs to prepare. Without preparation, we will sabotage the excellence that lies in the goal.

The year of 2018 was a season of preparation for me and I knew it because the Lord showed me the vision and directed me on what I needed to do. I only saw part of the picture, however, not the whole piece. The Lord only showed me part, I believe, as His way of motivating me and allowing me to build my faith in Him. My assignments and what God expected me to do to prepare for what He already had for me was very clear. Each step I took required seeking God in order for Him to reveal what to do next. As I got closer and closer to His expected end, I became clearer on what He was doing and how He was doing it. Here was my lesson through it all.

As an adolescent who struggled with anxiety, I had a pattern in my teenage years of becoming frustrated and easily angered in the process of preparation. In retrospect, I am now able to acknowledge that I had a fear of failure. What if things did not work out; what if I am wasting my time? Instead of detecting these thoughts and dealing with them when I was younger, I would lash out at people who were around me, and I was very sensitive to situations that were miniscule; they were a high trigger for me. My defense mechanism was displacement. I was concerned about the outcome of my situations, and I would express my feelings of concern by becoming angry and frustrated with people and other situations rather than confronting my fear; this was the part of me that God wanted to transform. Can you imagine what kind of adult I would be if I continued to throw tantrums when I was challenged and fearful of the end result of every situation?

Now that I am older and more mature, spiritually, I realize that in my youthful days, I did not appreciate the process of preparation, but I do now. In the phase of preparation, I am growing not only mentally but also spiritually. I am not entering in my established phase with pride, but rather, I am humbled by God's direction and prompting through the process. I have learned to depend on Him every step of the way and find meaning and purpose in my failures. He allows me to appreciate and value my destination as I realize that I did not make it on my own and it took a lot out of me to make it to where I needed to go. That which is buried on the inside of me is not realized outside of the journey, but rather through the journey. I've learned how self-determined and driven I am. I've discovered the strengths that I have and how much I am able to bear; not through my own strength and abilities, but through God. Some classify the stage of preparation as the wilderness journey. Through the wilderness journey, we are more equipped for our purpose.

I sat with a patient that I had treated for some time, and during a session wherein we were working on some goals that she wanted to accomplish, she disclosed that creating goals made her feel very nervous and anxious. As I probed further, she expressed the same exact thought patterns that I contended with as an adolescent: "What if things do not turn out the way I expect? I am afraid of disappointment." In that moment, I was able to relate to her and use my testimony to minister to her in a way that she could understand. If I never encountered these feelings and overcame, I would not be a success story to offer others hope. Ultimately, our journey is not about us, it is about those we can help along the way. We are not just preparing for our victories, but we are equipping ourselves to lead others to a place of victory.

We all encounter feelings of fear at times throughout our journey, and we will become discouraged and overwhelmed. Our defenses may overshadow our ability to clearly process our feelings. However, we do not want to stay in that place; it is defeat, not victory. As soldiers who encounter defeat during times of war, we have to regroup and determine a strategy for victory. Be aware of what your thoughts are and be mindful of where your thoughts should be versus where they actually are. Acknowledge your feelings and clearly define what that feeling is. Be transparent before God and look to Him for help in countering your thoughts and feelings. He will answer you and help you. Psalm 121:1–2 says, "I will lift up mine eyes unto the hills, from whence cometh my help. My help cometh from the Lord, which made heaven and earth." God is here to help us through the process, and at times He uses the process to get us closer to Him. Our ability to reframe our situations will assist throughout the process.

Spiritual Food for Thought:

Romans 8:30—Moreover whom he did predestinate, them he also called: and whom he called, them he also justified: and whom he justified, them he also glorified.

PERSONAL REFLECTION:

Question: What is the Lord preparing you for in this season of your life? What purpose do you feel you are called to function in?

Do not treat each trial as your first test. Think about how God has brought you out before, over and over and over. He did it then and He can do it now.

Exodus 17:1–7 speaks about the great miracle that God performed for the children of Israel when He directed Moses on how to respond to the need of the thirsty Israelites. God told Moses to smite the rock, and when he followed God's orders, water came from the rock and the children of Israel were able to quench their thirst. Despite the many miracles that God performed in the presence of the children of Israel, they had a pattern of doubting Him every time they were faced with a challenge. All that God did for the children of Israel was a sign that He was with them and cared for them deeply. Note that I classified these encounters as challenges, not problems.

Challenge is defined as "an objection or query as to the truth of something, often with an implicit demand for proof." Isn't God up for the challenge and isn't He well equipped? He wants to prove Himself and show that He will do exactly what He promised in His Word. Let us take a look at God's résumé.

In Genesis 17, God promised Abraham that his wife, Sarai, would have a son. It took a long time and the challenge for Abraham and Sarah was that they were advanced in age. In Genesis 21, Sarah gave birth to Isaac, the son of promise. God promised Abraham a son. He got it.

In 1 Samuel 16, God used Samuel to anoint David as king. However, David's process to becoming king came with great challenges. David encountered enemies from many different directions and had to contend with Saul, who was the king rejected by God. We see in 2 Samuel 5 that David became king over Israel when he was thirty years of age. God promised David that he would be king. He was.

In Exodus 6, God gave Moses a message for the children of Israel who were slaves in Egypt and under bondage by Pharaoh. The Lord told Moses in verse 6 of Exodus 6, "Wherefore say unto the children of Israel, I am the Lord, and I will bring you out from under the burdens of the Egyptians, and I will rid you out of their bondage, and I will redeem you with a stretched out arm, and with great judgments." The challenge for the Israelites and Moses is that Pharaoh's heart was hardened against the command of the Lord and he would not voluntarily release the children of Israel. Therefore, God brought much judgment on Pharaoh and the Egyptians. And as always, in the end God won. According to Exodus 12:51, "And it came to pass the selfsame day, that the Lord did bring the children of Israel out of the land of Egypt by their armies." God promised the children of Israel that He would deliver them from the bondage of Pharaoh. He did.

All throughout the Old Testament, there are prophecies and foreshadowing of Jesus Christ's birth, death, and resurrection. Isaiah 7:14 says, "Therefore the Lord himself shall give you a sign; Behold, a virgin shall conceive, and bear a son, and shall call his name Immanuel." Isaiah 53:12 says, "Therefore will I divide him a portion with the great, and he shall divide the spoil with the strong; because he hath poured out his soul unto death: and he was numbered with the transgressors; and he bare the sin of many, and made intercession for the transgressors." Psalm 49:15 says, "But God will redeem my soul from the power of the grave: for he shall receive me. Selah." All of these Scriptures are prophecies given that were fulfilled in the New Testament.

Matthew 1:20, 25 says, "But while he thought on these things, behold, the angel of the Lord appeared unto him in a dream, saying, Joseph, thou son of David, fear not to take unto thee Mary thy wife: for that which is conceived in her is of the Holy Ghost…. And knew her not till she had brought forth her firstborn son: and he called his name Jesus." God was in fact born of a woman, Mary, as was spoken in the Old Testament, and died on the cross for the sins of the world, which is detailed in Matthew 27. We glory not in the death of our Lord and Savior, but the resurrection. We have hope that as He fulfilled His assignment on earth and sits at the right hand of God in glory, so too we will live with Him in glory. Matthew 28:6–7 says, "He is not here: for he is risen, as he said. Come, see the place where the Lord lay. And go quickly, and tell his disciples that he is risen from the dead; and, behold, he goeth before you into Galilee; there shall ye see him: lo, I have told you." God promised the children of Israel a Messiah, and He came.

All these promises took time, but they surely came to pass. God is not in a rush; we are. God is not subject to time; He controls it. I noticed more keenly the value of a promise when I became a parent, and I also realized how heartbreaking it is when my toddler doubts my word. I would tell my three-year-old son, "After you have your dinner, you will get the ice cream you are asking for." Yet he cries and is saddened when he should be joyful that the time is coming when he will get exactly what he asked for. A delay in a promise is not a "no." But maybe my son is struggling with keeping his end of the agreement, finishing his dinner.

When God makes us a promise, He has no problem keeping His end of the deal, but what about our responsibility to keep our end of the covenant? Sometimes we delay the promises of God by our lack of obedience and commitment. Our walk with the Lord is a covenant relationship. There is an old hymn titled "Trust and Obey"; if you are not obeying, it will be difficult for you to trust.

Spiritual Food for Thought:

Isaiah 55:11—So shall my word be that goeth forth out of my mouth: it shall not return unto me void, but it shall accomplish that which I please, and it shall prosper in the thing whereto I sent it.

PERSONAL REFLECTION:

Question: What promises has God made to you? What parts of your character have been tested during your time of waiting, and how strong has your faith been on a scale of one to ten?

23

Are you a leader? Well, before you answer that question, ask yourself: 1) Do I get offended easily? 2) Do I take things personally? 3) How do I handle constructive criticism? And lastly, 4) Am I humble enough to be corrected?

As leaders, we are the first person seen and the first target of attack. Being a leader is not just a title, it is a position that is assigned to us for a purpose. So, when people discredit us, we should not get offended or take it personally. It is normal to have a human emotional response. But staying connected to God will help us to process and evaluate our feelings and emotions, and stay in line with God's Spirit in order to yield the right response.

Moses was a leader who was called by God. He had a passion for the people, which was a part of him that was recognized even before God called him and was also a part of the reason why God called him. He depended on God every step of the way, but when the people rose up against him, he took it personally, and instead of allowing God to handle certain matters, he handled them himself. Never feed off the energy of those you are leading; create and adjust the energy.

In Numbers 20, we see that the Lord specifically told Moses to speak to the rock that was to bring forth water for the thirsty Israelites. However, Moses was very frustrated by the complaining and murmuring of the children of Israel, and he struck the rock out of his anger and frustration. Moses misrepresented God. As leaders, we have to be reminded that we are positioned not in ourselves but in Him, and any confrontation that comes along the way of our journey is meant to test us so that we are aware of what our response will be. We are to give all confrontations to Him.

God challenges us to respond instead of react. The difference between a response and a reaction, according to *Psychology Today*, is that reactions are spontaneous and driven by biases, beliefs, and prejudices from the unconscious mind. Reactions are not processed cognitively as responses are. Reactions are part of our defense mechanisms. Responses, on the other hand, derive information from both our conscious and unconscious mind, and the process is slower rather than rash. The process of developing a response is very ecological, as it takes into consideration other people involved in the process and not just self. As leaders, we are expected to consider how others are impacted by our actions, and our responses allow us to consider others and make wiser decisions that we more than likely will not regret. God is calling us to be altruistic, just like He is.

We do not carry a title, we walk in a position. Titles are carnal, but positioning is spiritual. We at times think to ourselves, because we have a title, people must respect us or how dare people treat us with dishonor or disregard. But when we know our position and are secure in who we are in God, we are able to say to ourselves, "Whatever you do to me has to go through God first, and if He allows it, it is for my good." Frustration is present when peace is absent. Once you have peace in your position in God, you will not be frustrated by the actions and negative energy of others and you will not be moved to act out of character or out of the will of God. Because Moses acted out of character, he missed out on the blessing: entering into the Promised Land. Do not allow anyone to cause you to miss out on the blessings of God.

Throughout our leadership experience, we will have those who wish us well and want to see us grow. Their speech to us may not be soothing all the time. They will not agree with us all the time. But their positioning in our lives is necessary, and humility needs to be our disposition in order to receive what they have to offer. We should take the constructive criticism and be humble; it will work well for us in the end. When God has positioned you, He will make sure that you are cared for spiritually, emotionally, physically, and psychologically. Do not fight for yourself and become a defensive leader; let God fight for you and defend you. Channel your thoughts in the Word and be encouraged.

Spiritual Food for Thought:

Ephesians 4:26—Be ye angry, and sin not: let not the sun go down upon your wrath.

PERSONAL REFLECTION:

Question: What are some challenges that you experience as a leader around reactions and offenses? What steps can you take to address your identified challenge?

24

Our position of power is not purposed to create a dynamic of discomfort for others, but rather to pave the way of possibility and opportunities.

At times, we are challenged with the option to use our position of power to control and even to retaliate. When we struggle with unforgiveness and resentment and are privileged to have a position of dominance, we can at times use that dominance as an opportunity to retaliate. One of my favorite Bible characters of all times is Joseph. I appreciate and respect Joseph's character after experiencing betrayal and hatred from his biological brothers. Joseph was sold into slavery by his brothers after actually plotting to kill him due to jealousy. Joseph became the governor of Egypt, and when there was famine in every land including Canaan where his brothers and father lived, he had the power to retaliate, but he chose to extend mercy and hope. Joseph said to his brothers in Genesis 50:20, "As for you, you meant evil against me, but God meant it for good, to bring it about that many people should be kept alive, as they are today" (ESV). When we have the right perspective, the spiritual perspective, we will have the right response.

We should not use our position of power or our affiliation with those who are of the majority to create a feeling of discomfort for someone who is in an inferior position or is part of the minority. We should also not use our position to retaliate against those who have hurt us or people who look like those who've hurt us. At times, we fall into this way of functioning unconsciously due to our past experiences and also our current affiliations. It is also easy to take on the behavior of those we are around, and this in turn alters our way of thinking. Proverbs 13:20 says, "He that walketh with wise men shall be wise: but a companion of fools shall be destroyed."

Some people view power as their way of controlling situations and people, and this way of thinking is normal for some people. It may be a norm to some, but it is not a norm to God, and we will be held accountable for our actions. Therefore, God wants us to be aware. I love how God points out areas of our lives that go unchecked. He loves us that much to correct us and point us in the right path.

Second Corinthians 5:10 says, "For we must all appear before the judgment seat of Christ; that every one may receive the things done in his body, according to that he hath done, whether it be good or bad." Our mind is a part of our body and we must be sure to feed our mind with pure thoughts so we can be able to exhibit pure behaviors. So, I challenge you to be more mindful of your thoughts of others or anyone God has allowed you to interact with. If we are truly in God, know that everyone who God allows to cross our path is purposeful, whether their presence in our life is positive or negative. We cannot control the actions of others, but we can control our own behaviors. Joseph had no control over his brothers' actions in selling him into slavery. If he did, he would have turned everything around so that he would not have been sold into slavery. But what he did have control over was his response when he was promoted to his position of power. Joseph used his power for good, just as Esther did.

Let's take a quick look at the book of Esther. Esther was placed in a position of power after the fall of Queen Vashti. Haman was also elevated in his position with the king and used his power to threaten the lineage of Jesus Christ. Esther was in a position to preserve the lineage of Jesus Christ. At times, God will allow us to be placed in a position to experience a particular feeling that is related to how He will use us when the season arrives. Because Esther identified with the children of Israel, not only genealogically but also emotionally, God was able to use her connection to drive the need.

The Omniscient God, the One who knows all things, knew ahead of time that Haman would set out to destroy His people. Esther's position was for a purpose. She could have done two things: 1) disconnect herself from her people and bask in her power and prestige, with no regard for those who would be afflicted, or 2) recognize her calling and walk in her divine purpose. She knew that she was not purposed to create or support a dynamic of discomfort and oppression for others. She was created to pave the way of hope and salvation. Mordecai said to Esther in verse 13 and 14 of the fourth chapter of Esther, "Then Mordecai commanded to answer Esther, Think not with thyself that thou shalt escape in the king's house, more than all the Jews. For if thou altogether holdest thy peace at this time, then shall there enlargement and deliverance arise to the Jews from another place; but thou and thy father's house shall be destroyed: and who knoweth whether thou art come to the kingdom for such a time as this?" It is not about your power, it is about your purpose.

Spiritual Food for Thought:

Jeremiah 1:5—Before I formed thee in the belly I knew thee; and before thou camest forth out of the womb I sanctified thee, and I ordained thee a prophet unto the nations.

PERSONAL REFLECTION:

Question: In what capacity do you see yourself as powerful or influential? What is your challenge around feelings of resentment or unforgiveness, and how do you use your influence to act on your feelings?

25

Showing kindness and compassion to others can increase our level of empathy and compassion for ourselves. Our dissatisfactions with ourselves oftentimes lead to low self-esteem, self-blame, and unrealistic expectations.

When we lighten our expectations of others, it will have a direct impact on how we view ourselves. Expect only from God; He is the only one who will not let you down. I am reminded of a conversation that I had with a colleague of mine wherein I was venting about my expectations for an administrator who I worked with directly. Her words were so profound and resonated with not only my situation on the job but other familial and social relationships that increased my level of frustration. She said that I should not place expectations on others because it is not fair to them or to me. I will continue to be disappointed because they are not privy to what I am expecting of them, they are their own individual who functions very differently from me, and I have to allow others to be themselves. Well said and well received.

I not only changed my level of expectations for others, but I started to lighten up on how I blamed myself for things I did wrong. I started to say to myself, "You are entitled to make mistakes; mistakes help you to grow and become experienced and wiser; mistakes keep you human and allow you to see that without God, you can do nothing." My way of thinking about myself was directly impacted by how I thought of others. Changing my level of expectations for others also decreased conflicts that I had with people, which made me feel happier and less stressed.

As fallible human beings, we are prone to make blunders on our journey to perfection. If we do not sin and are perfected, then we are ready to go home to heaven. However, if we are still here, get used to falling. Proverbs 24:16 says, "For a just man falleth seven times, and riseth up again: but the wicked shall fall into mischief." When we fall, make mistakes, or sin, we are encouraged to correct our wrongs and keep moving; do not stay there. There is always a lesson that is learned in our fall, and the only expectation that we should have for ourselves and the Lord has for us is to learn the intended lesson.

Just as we are striving to be perfect and improve in areas of our lives, others are also on this same journey. In order to make it right, we have to experience and identify some wrong. It is, however, important for us to process our wrongs and learn valuable lessons from our mistakes. This part of the journey makes life more meaningful. We need God to be patient with us and, therefore, we need to practice patience with others. God is perfecting a work in us and in others. Being aware of thoughts of expectations for self and others is a great start to changing our thought patterns in this area.

Spiritual Food for Thought:

Psalm 118:8—It is better to trust in the Lord than to put confidence in man.

PERSONAL REFLECTION:

Question: What are your thoughts of expectations for yourself and others? What is your emotional reaction when you do not meet your own expectations and when others do not meet your expectations?

26

Why do we love? If we cannot love others, there may be a high possibility that we do not love ourselves.

Love is such a strong word, as it requires action to prove its validity and genuine quality. Do you really love me? How much do you love me? And what will I do to make you stop loving me? When we truly love someone, it is not because of what they do or do not do for and to us, but it is a choice that we make in our mind to be constant and committed to. If love was based on condition, we would fall in and out of it all the time. And if God's love was based on our acts or the lack thereof, we would be without hope. Romans 5:8 says, "But God commendeth his love toward us, in that, while we were yet sinners, Christ died for us." As a result of God's love, He gave of Himself. Not because of what we did or did not do but purely because of love.

In my marriage with my husband, I started the journey of really discovering how much I loved myself. In the beginning of our marriage, I blamed him for everything because he was right there in front of me, an easy target. We argued so often. I found a way to make my husband the focus of the problem for everything that frustrated me about myself and those around me, until I got to the point of being tired—tired of arguing; tired of avoiding what the real problem was; tired of myself and tired of my defense mechanism, displacement. God used and continues to use my marriage to change me. I realized there was no way for me to grow in life if I did not find a way to love myself and just love people. In order to love others, I had to find contentment within myself. Unresolved conflicts with self can lead to unexplained tension with others.

Tension, according to Dictionary.com, is a mental and emotional strain. Can you imagine being in this state with multiple people at a given time? No wonder people who struggle with unforgiveness look so unhappy and cannot find peace in their situations; tension is present. When you have peace and are content with yourself, it is so much easier to make amends and live at peace with others.

God has called us to love because He knows the level of tranquility that can be found in its presence. And because love is a verb, we are called to act on it. Every chance you get to show an act of kindness because of the love in your heart, act on it! James 4:17 says, "Therefore, to him who knows to do good and does not do it, to him it is sin" (NKJV). If God truly lives in your heart, He challenges you to respond in certain ways by simply putting a thought in your heart and mind. When you resist that thought of love or the opportunity to show love, you are resisting your own process of growth and release of tension.

If you truly love, I challenge you to act on it with everyone. We cannot choose who to love. John 3:16 says, "For God so loved the world that He gave His only begotten Son, that whoever believes in Him should not perish but have everlasting life" (NKJV). I oftentimes think about what my life would be like if God's love was subject to certain, selected people and I was not part of the chosen. Thankfully, I do not have to worry about that because His love is inclusive and constant. Therefore, our love to others should also be inclusive and constant.

Spiritual Food for Thought:

First John 4:20—If a man say, I love God, and hateth his brother, he is a liar: for he that loveth not his brother whom he hath seen, how can he love God whom he hath not seen?

PERSONAL REFLECTION:

Question: What are some unresolved conflicts you have with yourself? What part of you struggles with loving people due to these unresolved conflicts with self?

27

What are your thoughts of yourself as a result of rejection? Do you see yourself as insignificant, or less than others, despite your accomplishments?

I read a very profound message by Bishop T. D. Jakes, which gave me a clearer understanding as to why people tend to overlook people who they feel are insignificant. The truth is that their character is flawed. In the words of Bishop T. D. Jakes himself, "Nothing exposes character more than the way you treat people you don't think you need." This quote calls for a Selah moment. When I first read this quote, I thought of David and his process to becoming king.

When Samuel was sent to Jesse's house as the Lord commanded him, to anoint one of Jesse's sons as king over Israel, David was overlooked. When Jesse and his sons went to sacrifice, David was not even included. Samuel assessed Jesse's sons and thought based on their outward appearance they would be chosen by God, but none of them was chosen. The one who was disregarded and not invited was chosen by God, not man. First Samuel 16:7 says, "But the Lord said unto Samuel, Look not on his countenance, or on the height of his stature; because I have refused him: for the Lord seeth not as man seeth; for man looketh on the outward appearance, but the Lord looketh on the heart." In the process of being overlooked and disregarded, know that God has a purpose for your character. When you arrive at your destination of purpose, you will know how to find value in others, despite their current position or status in life.

Throughout my life, I remember periods of being overlooked. From what I could remember, through all my stages of life, there was some experience around being overlooked. According to research, support and motivation are fundamental for success and proper development. Not only support from parents but school administrators, teachers, family friends, coaches, and role models who see value in you and affirm you along the process to make you believe that you have potential to be great. Aside from my parents, I never had that constant support. Yes, it came from time to time from outside sources, but there was never any consistency. So, I struggled throughout my childhood to believe that I had potential. I rarely believed in myself. But God believed in me and was my constant cheer leader, even at times when I did not hear Him. He always made an open door and I cannot say that it was because of my potential; it was solely because of His grace.

When people do not see value in you, there is dishonor, disregard, and disdain. Here's the mindfulness practice that can help to prevent you from defining yourself by how people treat you. The enemy knows your purpose. His job is to break your spirit and demotivate you so you do not move into your divine purpose. He knows God's plan for you is great, and he will use people to try and abort your purpose as he tried to do with David. However, you now know his secret and can beat him at his own game. Use the mistreatment of others to mold your character, as Joseph did. Learn how to detect mistreatment and work harder to practice kindness, meekness, and humility; these are the qualities that you will need for your purpose anyway. So what the enemy meant for evil is actually working out for your good; God is using the enemy to birth some good character out of your experience. You win! The same people who overlooked you will eventually need you, and it is then that they will see how flawed their character is. Through that realization there will be hope for them to change.

Spiritual Food for Thought:

Genesis 50:20—But as for you, ye thought evil against me; but God meant it unto good, to bring to pass, as it is this day, to save much people alive.

PERSONAL REFLECTION:

Question: What are some of your experiences with rejection? How have your encounters affected you emotionally and shaped your self-esteem?

28

The way we treat others reflects our thoughts toward them. Our actions should be driven by love.

We may find that at times we get so caught up in our everyday functioning and behavioral habits that we do not take time out to think about how we are treating those around us. And maybe this is not a prioritized thought for some of us. We fall into the unconscious acts of treating people differently based on our thoughts toward them without realizing the behaviors we are exhibiting.

There are some people who we view as valuable or of importance. As a result of our thoughts we treat them with respect, we acknowledge them when they are in our presence, and we are sure to make them a part of our lives. Then there are those who we couldn't care less about. I know that this statement may sound harsh and not "Christian-like," but what are some of the ways we behave that send the message to others that, to you, they are not important? How do you respond to them when they are in your presence? If we take some time to think of the behaviors that we are exhibiting or even the behaviors that we are not exhibiting, then your question is answered. We are our greatest critics. We also know our thoughts more clearly than others do. First Corinthians 2:11 says, "For what man knoweth the things of a man, save the spirit of man which is in him? even so the things of God knoweth no man, but the Spirit of God." If our actions are truly telling what we are thinking, then we have a responsibility to address our behaviors and deal with those thoughts that are not "Christ-like."

The Word of God encourages us in Romans chapter 2 that God is not partial. God is not lenient with some based on their status quo and harsher with others based on their lack of talent and abilities, but He judges based on our status of keeping His Word. So, why is it that we as His followers do not the same? Instead, those who can benefit us in some way or another or have the ability to enhance our status and recognition are the ones who we esteem. Here is the unadulterated truth: we are all the same in God's eyes and our talents, abilities, and statuses mean nothing with Him; they are simply to enhance the kingdom of God. Therefore, everyone should be treated with value and esteem. If you fail to value anyone in the body of Christ, judge for yourself the reason why, challenge that thought with God's Word, and allow your mind to be transformed. If you do have thoughts of disregard and exhibit disparaging behaviors toward your brother or sister, it will be felt and noticed by them and that same dynamic will eventually be created in your surroundings.

God wants His church to grow wholesome and strong. God wants people to live in unity and find comfort in each other. God wants us to value each other the way He values us. God wants His people to be comforted. How privileged are we that He has chosen us to create these great dynamics. It is our responsibility to live up to the expectations of our creator. Let us do what He has created us to do; it is part of our purpose.

Spiritual Food for Thought:

Deuteronomy 1:17—Ye shall not respect persons in judgment; but ye shall hear the small as well as the great; ye shall not be afraid of the face of man; for the judgment is God's: and the cause that is too hard for you, bring it unto me, and I will hear it.

PERSONAL REFLECTION:

Question: Have you placed greater value on people based on their status quo or position? Analyze your interactions.

29

Are you content in whatever state you find yourself? If you are not, chances are, depression and anxiety are knocking at your door or have already been invited in.

Philippians 4:11 says, "Not that I speak in respect of want: for I have learned, in whatsoever state I am, therewith to be content." When you are not content, it breathes air of covetousness and jealousy. God will give you exactly what you need, not what you want. In Genesis chapter 13, we see the abundance that Abraham and Lot had, which led to strife between Abraham's herdsmen and Lot's herdsmen. Abraham knew that strife was not of God and opted to separate from Lot rather than live in a state of discord. Even though Abraham was older and could have chosen the land that he wanted, he humbled himself and took the lower seat; he allowed Lot to choose. Now the Word of God says in Genesis 13 that Lot looked at Sodom and saw how beautiful and fruitful it was and chose based on what he saw; Lot was covetous. Two of the synonyms for *covetous* are *grabby* and *selfish*. Yup, that was Lot. Lot could have had another response: "Well, Abraham, I came out with you and as a result of my connection to you, I was blessed beyond measure. I know you told me to choose, but I prefer for you to choose, and I will be content with what I get." But no, Lot allowed the lust of the eye to control his response and he chose Sodom. Lot put himself first rather than seeking out the best for Abraham. As a result, Lot got the land that he wanted but was not able to keep it. Abraham got what he needed and his contentment made him even more abundant.

The Lord told Abraham in Genesis 13:14–15, "And the Lord said unto Abram, after that Lot was separated from him, Lift up now thine eyes, and look from the place where thou art northward, and southward, and eastward, and westward: For all the land which thou seest, to thee will I give it, and to thy seed for ever." Notice that the Lord made this covenant with Abraham after Abraham's encounter with Lot and his submission to being content. The way we are created, the more we have the more we will want. And that is why God tells us to be content. Being content does not come naturally but requires work that takes place in our minds.

What are our thoughts as to what is valuable? People oftentimes place value on money and worldly possessions. However, if we are thoughtful of our purpose to build the kingdom of God through our service to His people, we would place more value on our service to the Lord rather than His service to us. When I say His service to us, I am speaking of all that which we expect God to do for us. "God, please bless me with that beautiful home You promised me" or "God, please bless me with that wealth You said I inherited and bless me with dominion and power to obtain that promotion because You said I should be the head and not the tail." Does this sound like some of our thoughts and prayers? Well, that used to be my kind of prayers and thoughts at one point in my Christian walk. Nevertheless, I am so happy that I got the right vision sooner rather than later.

When I first got saved, I thought that I finally would get to live the blessed, fruitful, "good" life. I would just ask God for things and He would bless me with everything good, which He really did, at first. I wanted a particular car, I would pray, and God would give me greater than I asked for. I needed money and I would ask Him and He would put it in someone's heart to bless me. I always gave Him thanks and was very mindful that it was Him, but I was never fully content. As life continued, I realized that my need or should I say "greed" got bigger and bigger and bigger. I was no longer satisfied with my current situation but always desired something more. The Lord brought me to a place of stagnancy for me to understand that He has to be enough to fill the void in me, not the things of this world or positions in this world. After I learned that lesson and learned it well, God moved me past my place of stagnancy and began a process of elevation, which required testing at each point to remind me that I need Him and everything I do is for Him. My desire for growth and promotion is now to be positioned for His glory and His service.

Spiritual Food for Thought:

Galatians 2:20—I have been crucified with Christ. It is no longer I who live, but Christ who lives in me. And the life I now live in the flesh I live by faith in the Son of God, who loved me and gave himself for me. (ESV)

PERSONAL REFLECTION:

Question: Do you find yourself in a place of being discontented with your accomplishments and possessions? How do you respond in your heart to people who have things or positions that you desire or aspire for?

Loneliness is a mental state and can be as intense as you allow. Turn your loneliness into solitude.

When people feel alone, they tend to believe that they are in their situations all by themselves. But we are not; God is always with us and has a purpose for our seasons of isolation. How can you navigate the feeling of loneliness to your benefit? Take your loneliness and transform it into solitude. What is solitude? According to *Psychology Today*, "Loneliness is marked by a sense of isolation. Solitude, on the other hand, is a state of being alone without being lonely and can lead to self-awareness."

There is growth in solitude! Solitude is necessary as it brings forth clarity in your mind, heart, and spirit. Take, for example, a library filled with noise and movement when you are trying to learn or study a topic of importance to your plans, whether it is an exam, a paper, an assignment, a book, or even personal research. The noise and movement presents distractions. There is a reason why the rule of all libraries is "no noise." Solitude is a place of peace and quiet where you can clearly hear God's voice and your own thoughts. He wants to tell you the next step or bring awareness to situations in your life that have been neglected for far too long. Take the time to listen; you need it and you deserve it. John 10:27 says, "My sheep hear my voice, and I know them, and they follow me." In order for us to be trained in knowing how to distinguish God's voice from any other voice, we need to be in solitude for a time. Stop and listen.

When is the last time you stopped and listened to your thoughts? When you do this, you have the power to discover who you really are. Leave the room of loneliness and go to that place of solitude. In every period of growth that I experienced, I can remember the sense of being all by myself. I never noticed this pattern before, but when I did, I began to appreciate it. Learning about self and experiencing growth is not very easy, and so, some people avoid listening to themselves and their thoughts and prefer to always be surrounded by distractions. This method of dealing with things in your life is avoidance, which is a defense mechanism.

A defense mechanism, according to Dictionary.com, is an unconscious mental process very much like denial, which is meant to protect an individual from impulses or thoughts that are hurtful or intolerable. What is so destructive about defense mechanisms is that they do not allow an individual to process that hurtful or intolerable impulse; they just perform this reoccurring dance that leads to further mental destruction and stagnancy. God has called us to be overcomers, and in order to overcome a situation, you have to first encounter it and confront it. Do not avoid your feelings and the impulses you are faced with; encounter it, deal with it, and overcome it.

Coping skills are beneficial, as they allow you to identify your feelings, acknowledge that they are present, and point out where your feelings originated. There are various kinds of coping skills, which work well for individuals. Finding the right one that works for you in your unique circumstances is key. Some people cope by meditating on the Word of God or singing an uplifting song that changes their negative way of thinking and ultimately their mood, whether it is depression, anxiety, or hopelessness. Learn to cope rather than be defensive; solitude will help you on your journey to discovery.

Spiritual Food for Thought:

Matthew 28:20—Teaching them to observe all things whatsoever I have commanded you: and, lo, I am with you always, even unto the end of the world. Amen.

PERSONAL REFLECTION:

Question: What have been your thought processes in regards to times when you felt abandoned by others who you expected to be there for you? What are some benefits of those isolated times?

Do you believe that you have the power to direct the course of your life?

We come back to our original thought. We have the power to influence our life course by mastering our thought process. When we think life, we will speak life. Vice versa, if we think death, we will speak death. The Word of God says in Proverbs 18:21, "Death and life are in the power of the tongue: and they that love it shall eat the fruit thereof." How can you speak with your mouth without first using your mind to think? The process first starts in your mind. So, if I think I am successful, I then speak successful words, which move me to behave and act successfully, pursue opportunities that will yield successful results, and make successful decisions that line up with my thoughts, ambitions, and goals. But I will go nowhere if I am not using my mind to think and allowing my heart to believe.

This process of success is driven by the power of the mind. To seal this deal, there is the power of God's Word. Deuteronomy 28:13 says, "The Lord will make you the head (leader) and not the tail (follower); and you will be above only, and you will not be beneath" (AMP). However, this promise is based on covenant. You have the responsibility to fulfill your end of the covenant. What is your part? The same verse goes on to say, "if you listen and pay attention to the commandments of the Lord your God." There is your part right there; your responsibility and commitment to the process of success and greatness in the Lord is to remain in Him and allow Him to direct the course of your life through obedience to His Word. He will lead you to that place of success and leadership/headship where you are called to be. Proverbs 16:3 says, "Commit thy works unto the Lord, and thy thoughts shall be established." Remember to commit everything in your thoughts and life to the Lord; no matter how big or small, He cares and wants to be involved. God wants us to experience success, and that is why He commanded us to make Him the main focus of our pursuits.

You may ask, how do I know that I am called to be a leader? How do I know that it is in my purpose to be great? Well, the answer is simple. God's Word says it. In Genesis chapter 1 verses 27–28, God said, "So God created man in his own image, in the image of God created he him; male and female created he them. And God blessed them, and God said unto them, Be fruitful, and multiply, and replenish the earth, and subdue it: and have dominion over the fish of the sea, and over the fowl of the air, and over every living thing that moveth upon the earth." We as God's people were created to rule and be great here on earth. My mother used to say all the time to me and my siblings when we were growing up, "You have to learn to dance at home before you can dance abroad." Meaning, in order for us to know how to act in public, we have to first practice at home. Earth is not our home, heaven is. However, for us to know how to walk in dominion when we get to heaven, we have to start practicing that level of authority here on earth. I challenge you to fully embrace the journey of success in God; it is rightfully yours.

The journey to success is not an easy journey, and sometimes people tend to give up because of their encounter with resistance or tension. However, both ingredients—resistance and tension—are needed in order to get the best results. Resistance and tension are only evidence that progress is in motion. Let us look at exercising and weight-lifting. In order for anyone to build muscles, there must be an increase in tension over a period of time. If a person's goal is to increase muscle growth, according to research, three primary mechanisms are used:

mechanical tension, metabolic stress, and muscle damage. Hearing this sounds very strenuous. Who wants to experience muscle damage on purpose? Well, a person who knows that the end result will be rewarding will be motivated to undergo the process.

The unique part of muscle atrophy is that you cannot lift the same amount of weights throughout your experience. There is a time when you have to increase the amount of weights you lift as you become comfortable with your regimen. Comfort is not part of your growth; resistance and challenge are the ingredients for the increase in your exercise goal and routine. To experience and encounter greatness, you must embrace discomfort, pain, and resistance. They will not be in your life for the long haul, but they are necessary in part of your journey to greatness.

Position yourself for God's will to be fulfilled in your life by structuring your thought process in line with God's Word. One of the greatest signs of humility is complete surrender. As you surrender to God, He will help you and guide you to where you are destined to be in Him. His plan for your life is very unique and special, created and designed specifically for you. This book is simply purposed to motivate you to get in position. Simply to remind you that God loves you and has great plans for you. Enjoy the journey. Embrace the challenges and bask in the glory that is waiting at the end, when you arrive to your expected end.

Spiritual Food for Thought:

2 Timothy 4:7–8—I have fought a good fight, I have finished my course, I have kept the faith: Henceforth there is laid up for me a crown of righteousness, which the Lord, the righteous judge, shall give me at that day: and not to me only, but unto all them also that love his appearing.

PERSONAL REFLECTION:

Question: Would you classify parts of your thought process to be life bearing or maladaptive? What steps can you make to change the parts of your thoughts that are maladaptive?

SCRIPTURAL INDEX

Matthew 28:20	(Day 30)	1 Corinthians 2:11	(Day 28)
Mark 8:34	(Day 20)	1 Corinthians 3:2	(Day 13)
Mark 8:36	(Day 20)	2 Corinthians 5:10	(Day 24)
Mark 11:25	(Day 15)	Galatians 2:20	(Day 29)
Luke 6:27-28	(Day 14)	Ephesians 1:4	(Day 5)
Luke 6:31	(Day 13)	Ephesians 4:26	(Day 23)
John 3:16	(Day 26)	Philippians 2:3	(Day 8)
John 6:63	(Day 1)	Philippians 4:8	(Day 8)
John 10:10	(Day 11)	Philippians 4:11	(Day 29)
John 10:27	(Day 30)	Philippians 4:13	(Day 5)
John 14	(Day 21)	Colossians 2:10	(Day 17)
Romans 2	(Day 28)	Colossians 3:2	(Day 7)
Romans 5:8	(Day 14; 26)	1 Thessalonians 5:18	(Day 19)
Romans 8:1	(Day 7)	2 Timothy 4:7-8	(Day 31)
Romans 8:28	(Day 5)	Hebrews 11:1	(Day 9)
Romans 8:30	(Day 21)	James 4:7	(Day 16)
Romans 12:2	(Day 5; 12)	James 4:17	(Day 26)
Romans 12:3	(Day 18)	1 John 4:18	(Day 8)
Romans 12:15	(Day 13)	1 John 4:20	(Day 26)

ABOUT THE AUTHOR

Latoya A. Delmadge is a licensed social worker and doctoral student who specializes in individual and family therapy. Latoya has practiced in the field of social work for over eight years and desires to use her skills to further the kingdom of God and support individuals in cognitive-related struggles that keep them bound, using effective evidence-based practice, mainly mindfulness, cognitive behavioral, and solution-focused therapy. Through professional trainings, research, and everyday practical experience in working with patients, God has given Latoya insight into the way the mind works and how our thinking affects the way we feel and respond to people and situations around us, which in turn shapes our lives.

Latoya is happily married to Albert C. Delmadge III, and together they have two beautiful children: Aaron Levi Delmadge, who is four years old, and Avia Jazleen Delmadge, who is two years old. Albert and Latoya believe in teaching their children mindful, biblical principles and more importantly aim to model acceptable behaviors and rewarding responses to life circumstances.

Latoya is the daughter of David and Maxine Reid, who are ordained pastors and have taught her how to labor in the kingdom of God. Latoya is also covered by her second parents, Bishop and Pastor Delmadge, who oversee Christian Heritage Ministries in Brooklyn, New York; Kissimmee, Florida; and Ghana.

Professionally, Mrs. Delmadge has worked with patients diagnosed with depression, anxiety, and bipolar disorder, and the way patients use one of the strongest organs in their body, the mind, has been the bulk of the work in treatment. Latoya functions as a clinical director for Community Counseling and Mediation in Brooklyn, New York, and serves faithfully her staff and patients. Latoya is also a major support to her husband, who is a full-time pastor for Christian Heritage Ministries in Brooklyn, New York.

Having a spiritual and psychological understanding of how the mind works, Latoya has dedicated her work to educating patients on how to cope with depressive and anxious symptoms through the medium of combating maladaptive thoughts.

Latoya realized how much Christians struggle with maladaptive thoughts, which can be seen in personality disorders and a lack of spiritual growth. Through education and awareness, Latoya has worked with many believers to recognize patterns of unhealthy behaviors that have left people in a state of stagnancy and unhappiness.

Latoya understands the various channels to reach people and provide awareness, and through God's leading, she wrote this book with hopes to shift the thinking patterns of her readers and create a space to be more reflective and self-aware of how and why we think the way we do.

Latoya greatly desires to add to the field of social work and mental health through a spiritual channel as research proves that spiritual practices and belief systems are effective in addressing mental health concerns.

To contact Latoya Delmadge, feel free to send an e-mail: mindfulproverbs@gmail.com

CPSIA information can be obtained
at www.ICGtesting.com
Printed in the USA
BVHW031224010419
544230BV00009B/838/P

9 781946 453594